POSTERS OF THE FIRST WORLD WAR

POSTERS OF THE FIRST WORLD WAR

selected and reviewed by Maurice Rickards

EAM EVELYN, ADAMS & MACKAY

First published 1968 by Evelyn, Adams & Mackay Ltd
9 Fitzroy Square, London W1. All rights reserved
Designed by Maurice Rickards, MSIA
Text printed letterpress by The Camelot Press, Southampton
Illustrations printed offset by Alfieri & Lacroix Editore, Milan
Bound in England
S.B.N. 238 78825 3

The 1914 war was Man's first big exercise in systematic destruction. It was carried out at first tentatively, with occasional reference to traditional chivalries—then, as these gave way to the realities of economics, boldly. In its later phases it relied heavily on force of numbers. In the end it was realised that victory would come not from an audacious master-stroke, not from courage or daring, not even from some surprise technology, but from resolute acceptance of withering numerical losses. It became a matter of population statistics.

As an exercise in destruction it cannot be said to have failed. Working largely on a basis of trial and error, it used up men, money and morale on a scale never before recorded.

Classically defined either as 'limited' or 'absolute' according to the scale of its objective, war can be a relatively self-contained incident or an all-out frenzy. It was Clausewitz who pointed out that there is a tendency for all wars, however limited their original aim, to become absolute if belligerents are equal in power and tenacity. Clausewitz was right. The balance of power and tenacity in the First World War was enough to last more than four years and to ring up a world total of 30 million killed and wounded, with an additional figure of 30 million civilian casualties as incidentals. Even the generals were surprised.

With their feet firmly planted in the stirrups of the nineteenth century the generals had taken too little account of the passage of time. There had been no European war for nearly half a century. But during that time the breech-loading rifle had become a magazine rifle and the magazine rifle had become a machine-gun. In the face of the machine-gun, men got off their horses and dug into the earth. 'Trenches' arrived.

As far back as the American Civil War it had happened; in place of the spirited cavalry dashes and the cut-and-thrust of a war of movement, there had emerged a war of attrition and exhaustion. It was industrialised warfare. Men and materials were conveyor-belted to relatively static points of delivery—raw materials to a destruction line. New developments in railway transport allowed supply and maintenance from a safe distance; with techniques of defence far outstripping those of attack there developed a situation of mutual ineffectiveness—a stalemate of equal and opposite forces in permanent collision.

The principle was still a novelty. Within the recollection of many of Europe's senior war professionals there had been not only cavalry charges but close infantry formations volleying alternately at command, and mutually agreed battle-pitches to avoid civilian suffering. Barbed wire, dug-outs and firing steps, mutual saturation of static positions by high-explosives—these were not yet in the rule-book.

In less than six weeks of the opening of the 1914 war, two of the largest armies mankind had ever mustered came face to face in a more or less continuous line from Switzerland to the North Sea.   There were two million men on each side.   The first six weeks of action had been just about the last of the old-style warfare in Europe.   Then the armies dug in.   It was the beginning of the long nightmare.

As one historian puts it, 'Without room to manœuvre, and thus condemned to frontal attacks, for more than four years the neo-Napoleonic generals who had despised fortification, failed to solve the problem in siege warfare set by modern fire power, especially by the machine-gun, combined with trenches and barbed wire.   Notwithstanding delusive instances in which success repeatedly seemed within reach, every assault finally failed in mud and blood.   Attempts to crush the defensive by multiplying guns and shells finally resulted in bombardments so severe that assaulting troops themselves could not advance across the chaos of shell craters.'

It was a situation that nobody had anticipated.   Soldiers, generals, politicians—all of the participants, whatever their status, whatever their nationality, had gone into the war on a strictly short-term basis.   In Britain the popular phrase had been 'all over by Christmas'; this, the jaunty view of the ordinary man, was no more than an expression of the universal official attitude.   For all of the belligerents, each unable to support the economic burden of a long-drawn fight, it was a built-in requirement that it should in fact—quite literally—all be over by Christmas.

As though mesmerised by the universal acceptability of a short war, all of the countries concerned prepared for it; each of them conceived the course of operations as a predetermined programme.   Regardless of imponderables, and often without reference to friends and neighbours, the plan of campaign of each general staff was cut and dried.   It was like a gigantic peace-time 'manœuvre', with universal participation, insufficient consultation, live ammunition, and casualties for keeps.

But it went wrong.   The Schlieffen Plan, which would almost certainly have succeeded if it had been carried out according to the script, was modified.   German chief-of-staff Von Moltke, to whom had fallen the legacy of Schlieffen, added trimmings to the plan, bringing in off-the-cuff inventions as he went along.   The result confused everybody.   By Christmas, instead of being over, the war had produced Mons, the Marne, and Ypres; it had produced a ragged and uncertain Eastern Front; most significantly of all, it had produced a 500-mile dig-in half across Europe. This had not been the idea at all.

Moltke's were by no means the only mistakes.   At every hand, at every level, there was misjudgment, muddle and inadequacy; military leaders in virtually every one of the belligerent countries failed to foresee the implications of the war and to adjust their thinking to the new conditions of the new technology.   They floundered their way through, accepting gigantic losses, covering up misjudgments, indulging their personal vanities and tantrums, bickering with colleagues, military superiors and political masters—and empirically flinging in additional hundreds of men by way of statistical make-weight. Of all the great names of the time—Haig, Moltke, Foch, French, Ludendorff, Rupprecht—none was without his burden of weakness, none entirely free of unreadiness, of duplicity, of self-deception. Their mistakes were among the most costly in the whole of human history.

So far as the general public was concerned (and this includes the general public in the trenches) these men were unassailable. Singly and collectively they were screened by the fog of war—the official fog of censorship and secrecy. In the name of military security the scale of their mistakes remained unseen. Only in the lengthening casualty lists did their misjudgments begin to show. Publication of the lists soon stopped; the time came when it was not merely a case of not publishing the figures—they were rigidly concealed. And even when the scale of disaster became too obvious to overlook, when the generals had used up all their credibility, they were replaced not for inefficiency but 'for more onerous duties' in other fields. It was imperative that the mystique of leadership be unimpaired. The fog of war prevailed.

The magnitude of the catastrophe that had befallen everybody was difficult to grasp, even for those who knew the truth. The war had gone wrong, wrong so spectacularly and irreparably that there was no one who could see a way out.

It was a trap that now contained millions. They confronted each other beneath a mutual hail of death. Between them lay the mud of no-man's-land, the sump of their destruction—the shattered stumps of trees and human limbs, the rat-infested hulks of horses, the nameless shreds that hung from barbed wire.

'Nothing in history,' says one writer, 'is more astonishing than the endurance, patience and good humour so generally shown by the great masses of hastily trained civilians from all the great countries engaged. In former campaigns, except during the comparatively rare incidents of battle, troops were generally withdrawn from the immediate contact of the enemy and immune from danger. In the Great War a large proportion of the total forces were continually standing over against each other in trenches sometimes a bare thirty yards apart. In dangerous sectors such as Ypres the normal wastage of a battalion acting as trench garrison would be at least twenty men a day. Men would live for long spells under conditions fouler and more horrible than the beasts. . . . The actual losses in battle far exceeded any proportion known to modern warfare. It had been calculated that no unit could maintain any fighting efficiency if its casualties exceeded 50 per cent. In all the great battles, however, such a loss was often and greatly exceeded. Battalions would constantly emerge with one or two officers and less than a hundred men, to be thrown after remaking within six weeks or two months into a no less consuming furnace. . . .'

It was to this consuming furnace, in a score of languages, but with striking similarity of visual impact, that the world's war posters invited the civilian public's attention.

In a world without radio and television, and where newspapers were still the preserve of a literate minority, the poster was the one big instrument of mass communication. It was a medium that was accepted and understood by the public at large; it was tried and tested—and it was cheap. All over Europe, and indeed throughout the world, the poster had taken its place in the economy of distribution. Industrialisation, with its twin corollaries of mass production and mass consumption, had harnessed the poster to mass persuasion. In the great new world of the turn of the century there was scarcely a product or a service that had not had the poster treatment. For popular impact and proved effectiveness, the poster was out on its own.

It had the added advantage, among the gentry, of a certain respectability. Since the time of Chéret, and increasingly since Toulouse-Lautrec (whose posters had brought to the medium the *cachet* of 'fine art') there had grown up a poster-fancying cult. People collected posters. There were poster sales; there were poster exchanges, poster societies and poster fanciers' magazines.

Like new old-masters, some posters had a specific market value. Lists of current prices appeared; sometimes there were even black-market posters, filched from the stock-in-trade of the bill-posting companies. It had not been so very long ago, in the heyday of Mucha and Lautrec, that people had stripped off freshly pasted posters before the paste had had time to set. Thus it was that the poster commanded the attention not only of the rank and file but of the *literati* as well. As an all-round instrument of persuasion, for governments anxious to keep their people on the boil, the poster was the obvious choice. It had served a long apprenticeship. In 1914 it came of age.

As country after country came in, the poster population grew; in each area it appeared in clearly discernible phases. The pattern followed a logical sequence. It was the sequence of warfare itself.

First there was the call for men and money—basic ingredients of war. For most of the belligerents, with conscription a longstanding institution, just one poster took care of the men. This was a proclamation of mobilisation. It required no pictorial impact and no persuasive slogan. Money was different; currency was less easily mobilised; for this there was a

8

burgeoning of poster blandishment—appeals for war loan subscriptions, war funds and charities of every description. The raising of money was a priority, not only initially, but throughout the war as coffers drained and Loan succeeded Loan. Defence Loans, War Loans, Victory Loans, Freedom Loans—with or without evocative titles, with or without emblazoned percentile inducements [95],* the call for money was continuous.

Second phase, as the war got going, was the call for help for the fighting man, for comforts for the troops and sacrifice on the home front. This covered everything from Tobacco Funds to injunctions to save wine for soldiers.

Third phase was the call for help for the wounded, the orphans and refugees. This phase was finely judged in its timing; it was withheld for long enough to avoid premature despondency and yet appeared soon enough to convey official recognition of sacrifice. It was generally exploited as an incentive to more sacrifice. Wounded soldiers served to jolt the civilian conscience.

Increasing shortage, both of men and of materials, produced the next phase. Here came the call for women to work in the factories, for increased munition production, for saving of vital materials, economies in food consumption and increased austerity all the way round.

A recurrent theme, emerging at strategic points throughout the pattern, is the appeal for a last overwhelming effort, one further subscription to a War Loan, a final crushing blow at a flagging enemy. The appeal for money is linked to virtually anything that forms the immediate topic of concern, whether it be munitions production, the 'shortening of the war', gratitude to the dead and wounded, or the last vital stroke.

Whatever the language, whatever the country, this is the universal pattern; this is the basic structure of the apparatus of persuasion. It is here that we see the most significant of the many points of identity that pervade the posters of the belligerents. In the universality of its images, in its multilingual guardian-angels and dragon-killers, in its archetypes of good and evil and its invocations of nobility and righteousness, the poster approach of every country shows resemblances that are inescapable. But in the overall identity of pattern there emerges a more basic likeness—a common strategy that links all to all. If the events that led up to the war had overtones of a Greek tragedy, in which all of the participants seemed to be playing out predestined roles—if the war itself bore signs of universal conspiracy, the pattern of its poster history shows a unity no less striking.

In the observance of this pattern, almost alone among the exceptions was Great Britain. Unlike continental Europe, which for centuries had accepted the principle of compulsory military service, Britain relied—in

* *Numbers in brackets refer to illustrations.*

peace or war—on volunteers. Her efforts to raise an army of some millions of men by means of posters was a source of amazement to friends, neighbours and enemies alike. It was nearly a year and a half before Britain finally settled for full-scale call-up.

With a dislike for compulsory soldiering that bordered, some said, on the pathological, the British had always relied on a small professional army, a navy to get them to where the fighting was, and a sense of security built on the seas between. When it began, the 1914 war was viewed in much the same light as the South African Campaign: this was something that the Army could look after as part of its normal job. They were 160,000 men—enough to fill a large football stadium. To the cheers of the populace, including some millions of males of 'military age', they marched off to do their job. For those who stayed behind it was Business as Usual.

With a dislike for advertising that also bordered on the pathological, Britain approached the business of advertising for an army. Kitchener had been impressed with the results of a small press advertisement which, greatly daring, the Army had tried shortly before the war. It was headed, beneath the royal coat-of-arms, *Your King and Country Need You*, and it finished off with the words *God Save the King*. Kitchener advocated changing the heading to *Lord Kitchener Needs You*—and trying it again. (Kitchener insisted that Army advertising should always sign off with God Save the King.)

But publicity began in earnest with the formation of the Parliamentary Recruiting Committee. Under its aegis there appeared a series of posters that was eventually to scrape the bottom of the barrel of persuasion. As graphic art—even as British graphic art—it was outstandingly undistinguished. As propaganda it was often painfully inept. But throughout the gigantic battles of 1914 and 1915, through the Marne, Ypres, Neuve Chapelle, through the German gas attacks and the Franco-British offensive of Champagne and Loos, it filled the gaps in the British trenches. By the time conscription came it had helped to raise a million men—of whom nearly half had been killed or wounded.

The campaign had started off with pictorial bugle calls, but the appeal to simple patriotism was soon exhausted. As poster followed poster in increasing numbers, there were finally few persuasive twists that were not tried.

At levels that ranged between the naïve and the near-satanic, with ever-increasing insistence the civilian male was needled. It shortly became a matter of mobilisation by shame. *Daddy, what did you do in the Great War?* [46] says an indiscreet little girl to her ulcerating father in years to come, as a son and heir plays soldiers at their feet. *Will you go, or must I?* [39] demands an Irish girl of her unmobilised man; in the background, clearly marked with the name, Belgium burns. Said a letterpress poster,

Have you a reason, or only an excuse? This was the level at which most of the posters of the Parliamentary Recruiting Committee were pitched. With a voice rising almost to a squeak, the campaign suffered from a mounting loss of dignity; it never fully overcame the disadvantage of its continual reminder of the presence of 'shirkers' and 'slackers'— evidence of its own defeat.

The appeal to women as recruiting agents was by no means oblique: *If your young man neglects his duty to his King and Country, the time may come when he neglects his duty to YOU* [23]. And, coming frankly into the open: *TO THE WOMEN OF BRITAIN—won't you help and send a man to join the Army today?* The role of the female as government spokesman, whether as wife, sweetheart, mother, daughter, or battlefield guardian angel, was common to the war effort of all the belligerents; it was in Britain in the first eighteen months that it had the longest and hardest run. It was also in Britain, generally speaking, that the artwork was worst.

Other British posters of the period appealed to straightforward self-interest *(It is far better to face the bullets than to be killed at home by a bomb* [15].*)* Others adopted a jaunty heartiness; one design showed three soldiers playing cards in the trenches: *Will you make a fourth?* Another had a khaki-clad Irishman appealing to his countrymen: *COME ON! Don't spoil a good fight for want of men to win it!* Others again, like the cavalryman *(Forward to Victory)* invoked a nineteenth-century death-or-glory glamour [85].

One German commentator, squinting slantwise at the British recruiting effort, was genuinely shocked at these gambits; he permitted himself to wonder whether 'troops drummed together by such crude methods can be the right material to stand the rigours of war for any length of time'. There was a general impression (not only in Germany) that you ought not to try to raise an army by the means that you use for selling soap-flakes. (As it turned out, recruiting methods appeared to make little difference, either to the capacity of soldiers to withstand rigours over a length of time, or to the territorial gains and losses that their resolution cost. In the three-and-a-half years that followed the Aisne, the battlefront in the West is reported to have shifted to and fro over a distance of rather less than ten miles.)

It must be said that the British poster scene was not wholly unredeemed. Alfred Leete (whose other claim to immortality was a trade-mark figure for a beer firm) came up with a novelty—Lord Kitchener himself [6]. *Your country needs YOU* is by no means a major work, but its posterly simplicity has impact far in excess of any of its contemporaries. His lordship's accusing finger has haunted Britons since they first saw it. It is the archetype of all wartime father figures, crib-source for a host of mimics.

Like the man himself—brooding, compulsive, and final—it has entered into the mythology of the nation; it has become a trade-mark figure for World War I. In a multitude of contexts, sacred and profane, it has been revived in parody. In the wave of mock-nostalgia that swept the last of the nineteen-sixties, the image was again revived—this time as a pop-art decoration piece. Kitchener, killed at sea in the summer of 1916, would have been greatly mystified.

It would be churlish to minimise Leete's success with the Kitchener design, but it must be conceded that the mediocrity of the British poster approach threw even moderate competence into prominence. Like logical civil servants, those who commissioned recruiting posters left the choice of artist largely to the experts—the printers. This was no time for the long-haired pros and cons of artistic merit. This was no time, even, for having posters designed by poster artists. If printers didn't understand these matters, then who did? The result was a remorseless flow of pernickety coloured drawings from printers' 'art departments'. *WHO'S ABSENT? Is it You?* [11] (described in a Government poster catalogue as 'a striking John Bull poster which hit the mark') is typical.

In his personal memoirs, Arthur Gunn, printer of many of Britain's recruiting posters, reveals their casual origins. Writing some twenty years afterwards, he says, 'We printed about 43 different ones, all of which were my own ideas. I used to conceive an idea for recruiting, get a sketch made myself by our own artist . . . and take it round to No. 11 Downing Street. If they liked it, no one else could stop it. One particularly successful poster was entitled *Daddy, what did you do in the Great War? . . .*'

An exhibition of German and Austrian industrial art, mounted in London shortly after the war began, failed to make the least impression on the British visual way of life. The exhibits had the disadvantage not only of being 'foreign'—but 'enemy alien'. Said the editor of a London poster magazine, 'It would not have been disadvantageous to have chosen some other example than the German one and thus to have avoided an association that at present is peculiarly unfortunate. . . . It is not going too far to call a great deal of Munich-made poster art squat, ugly, lowering and decadent.' Calling for encouragement for those English designers who express their feelings 'in a free, bright, natural and taking manner', the writer warned that 'heavy eccentricity may count its admirers in dozens, but healthy naturalism counts its friends in millions'.

An exhibition in Berlin, put on in aid of the German Aeronautic Fund, showed Berliners a glimpse of British recruiting posters. 'The exhibition is a great material success,' said a German news report, 'notwithstanding the general disappointment at the poor and inartistic designs.' It was a comment almost certainly more in sorrow than in hate.

It was a comment that was not without an echo in Britain. Almost to a man, those few among British artists who had had poster experience were ignored. Frank Brangwyn and Gerald Spencer Pryse, neither of them poster artists in the generally accepted sense, but whose work had occasionally appeared on pre-war poster hoardings, were brought in by a side door. Commissioned by Frank Pick, general manager of London's Underground Railways, both of these artists produced poster-drawings for display on railway stations. The drawings were conceived strictly as morale builders; they carried little in the way of wording and relied for their impact almost entirely on the driving sincerity and conviction that infused them. Here was a striking change from the soapy superficiality of printers' art departments. Here was genuine emotion, a first-hand involvement in the war, the raw and urgent energy of men convinced.

Pryse, a man of deep social conscience, was in Antwerp when the war began. As a despatch rider for the Belgian Government he had intimate knowledge of the effects of the German thrust through the country; his lithographs—carried out on slabs of limestone that he humped about in a motor-car—were heat-of-the-moment war reports.

Brangwyn—also, as it happened, with Belgian connections—was a Welshman born in Bruges. Well known long before the war for his uncompromising realism, his renderings of the truth of war had massive impact.

If Britain, with her *Hurry up, Boys* approach [2], was at first an exception to the general pattern, if in the mediocrity of her ordinary poster standards she was second even to America, in Brangwyn and Pryse at least she spoke in the common voice of the world's artists. Perhaps nowhere else is the universality of that voice as clearly demonstrated as in a comparison of Brangwyn's army-orphanage family group and the German family group of Hönich. Here, not only in subject matter, not only in compassion and conviction, but also even in details of style, there is an identity of feeling that links them for all time. While the Brangwyn treatment tends on the whole to a greater ruggedness of texture, there are points of resemblance that are almost uncanny. It is difficult to believe that the detail of the woman's head and hand from the Hönich poster is not vintage Brangwyn. It is perhaps unlikely that Brangwyn of London and Hönich of Munich ever actually met, but here, in these two posters, they come face to face. Brangwyn's wartime work—including many of his war posters—was given the honour of a 7-page illustrated article in Germany's poster magazine *Das Plakat*. This, while battles raged along the Western Front, was a significant tribute.

Britain's reactions to Brangwyn's work were distinctly less appreciative. According to many well-informed Britons, his drawings were quite unsuitable. Not only were they, as one commentator expressed it, 'too artistic', they had the additional demerit of 'showing the seamy side of war'. Of Brangwyn's *To Arms* drawing [17] he said, 'The motives that make a man enlist nowadays are many and varied. Those that keep back the man who *ought* to enlist are, I believe, first, lack of knowledge of the need, and, second, *fear* in some form or another—not so often actual fear of death, I believe, as fear of the discomforts and hardships of the soldier's life. Such a poster as this one by Mr. Brangwyn tends to emphasise the latter rather too much.' It was clearly desirable that, whatever else it did, the recruiting poster should not permit itself to pierce the fog of war.

(We may note in passing that the poster in question was in fact only a remnant. It was a surviving right-hand section of a larger drawing. The original, as it first appeared under the unofficial auspices of the Underground Railway Company, showed a group of figures to the left of the pointing soldier. Both the bisection of the picture, with its resultant imbalance, and the super-exclamatory slogan, are the work of another hand. 'Adaptation' of an artist's work—as maltreatment of this kind was called—was by no means rare, either in Britain or elsewhere. But then, as everybody said, there was a war on.)

In spite of the brutality of his *Put Strength in the Final Blow* drawing [67] —certainly one of the most vicious posters that the war produced— Brangwyn's *forte* was in the depiction of the 'seamy side'. Among his total of some three dozen war posters, the large majority dealt with compassion for misfortune, whether it was comfort for the troops, refugee aid, care for the wounded, or funds for orphans. Like Pryse, Brangwyn also drew straight on to the stone; signed copies from limited editions of his lithographs fetched high prices, not only among poster-fanciers, but among art buyers all over the world.

The work of Brangwyn and Pryse was in the grand tradition of European lithography. Like much of the pictorial material that appeared on war posters, it was not strictly speaking poster art. As with Toulouse-Lautrec and the poster founding fathers, the medium merely offered a wider dissemination of work that was normally the province of the few. Francisque Poulbot in Paris (whose money-collecting children for the *Journée du Poilu* [47] was but an extension of his normal urchin drawings), Max Antlers in Berlin [199], Hans Friedrich in Leipzig [70], Wallace Morgan in New York [233]—these artists merely switched their subjects to the national effort. Often their drawings became posters by the simple addition of wording, top or bottom. Sometimes they even left the lettering to the printer. Still working on stones that weighed anything up to a thousand pounds (special trolleys and lifting gear were used to handle them) they moved out of the nineteenth century into the war.

The advent of lithographic zinc and aluminium—hastened outside Germany by the cutting-off of supplies of Bavarian limestone—gave a new impetus to a medium that had been, to say the least, cumbersome. But the true lithographers stayed with the stone. In art museums all over the world, often as fractured and punished as the printers who heaved them about, their original slabs are preserved.

Lithography is a medium admirably suited to the dash and urgency of the war drawing. In the posters that exploit it there is a sense of personal commitment, a sense of actuality and immediacy that the more formalised styles of other media lack. For the auto-lithographers, it was as personal as handwriting.

It was by no means always the artist himself who carried out the finished drawing. The obsessive muscularity of the Brangwyns was rare. More often than not, in the days before photographic copying came in, original drawings were laboriously copied on to the stone by hand, line by line and dot by dot, by printers' craftsmen. But the spontaneity of the original remained; with its intimate air of contact between the spectator and the subject, with its subtle control of under- and over-statement, and with—above all—its sense of authority, it carried conviction. In the *On les aura!* poster by Faivre [5] there is more to its impact than dramatic simplicity, more than just the dynamic and expression of the figure—there is the very texture of communication, the instant touch of chalk to paper, the touch of truth.

It is this driving quality of truth that infuses many of the posters of World War I, whichever side they fought on. It is present in Max Antlers' *Soldatenheime an der Front* [199], in the *Grande Matinée de Bienfaisance* [142] by Lucien Jonas, in Fouqueray's *Songez aux foyers détruits* [156], and in the tragic figure of the machine-gunner in the British prisoner-of-war poster [212]. It is a touch that admits of no dissimulation; the smooth heroics of guardian angels, the set-piece glory of a Boy-Scout sword-bearer, the studied simplicity of a U-boat commander—these all too clearly reveal the art that conceals their art. Whether we are belligerent or neutral, connoisseur or layman, with these we are on our guard. They are contrivances; they may, or may not, be credible. With the Brangwyn/Antlers/Fouqueray approach, we feel there is no shadow of a doubt: all this is *real*. It is only when the technique so far forgets itself as to stray into stylisation that it fails; the head of Hindenburg [223], even apart from its anatomical oddity, is unforgettably unreal. In its evocation of monuments and medallions it is a reality twice removed from truth.

The lithographic approach, with its continual harking back to limestone and its exploitation of the individual 'handwriting' of the artist, was by no means the only successful poster idiom. If Britain saw only the alternatives of the fairground and the Royal Academy, other countries saw other ways. In Germany particularly (and indeed in Germany mainly) there had come into existence a poster form that stood aside from both these streams; it was destined to steal the poster scene for half a century. With Europe's hoardings still largely dominated by picture-book posters it had come as a refreshing change.

It had long been grasped—back even before the turn of the century—that one of the primary requirements of the poster was simplicity. Each in his own idiom, artists explored the possibility of leaving things out. Each sought to present a strikingly dominant major feature (more often than not a figure) with elimination of everything that was not essential to the transmission of the message. In this evolutionary process, many designs had reached a high level of refinement. Typical of the principle was Faivre's *Versez votre Or* [52]. Here was the attainment of the irreducible minimum, greatest impact for least fuss—poster perfection. The isolation of the essential elements, their unmistakable relationship as the coin bears down upon the man, the visual pun of the pecking cockerel, the novelty of the proposition that the message communicates (that the enemy can literally be beaten by money)—these are the ingredients of success. But the actual rendering is still in terms of turn-of-the-century lithography. From Germany came the next big step.

It could really be said to have started in 1906, when the first of the Hohlwein posters appeared. Ludwig Hohlwein brought to the poster a new kind of simplicity—a simplicity not only of commission and omission, but of visual rendering. With an eye that saw the world as a simple statement of tone and colour, he dismissed the lithographic texture and the 'pencil sketch'; he entered a new world of vision.

His poster for the internee exhibition in Switzerland [216] is typical. With its ruthless tonal separation and its convincing suggestion of three-dimensional form Hohlwein's work had all the simplicity and compulsion of 'pencil-sketch lithography'—with the added impact of commanding colour-masses. Other artists before him had experimented with the attention-value of flat colour areas, but the effects had been frankly two-dimensional. The Beggarstaff brothers in England, only a few years before, had produced posters of a revolutionary simplicity with cut-out coloured paper; by its virtuosity and audacity their design technique had set the poster world by the ears, but for all the professional acclaim that their work aroused, it failed with the general public; it lacked the three-dimensional realism that people were used to. It was 'artist's stuff'. With Hohlwein it was artist's stuff—but it looked real as well; it appealed to every level of visual sensibility.

Hohlwein started his career as an architect. The poster genius within him lay low through his student years, through his work in interior décor (he designed the refreshment room in Munich's big department store and 'modernised' the Hotel Continental) and through his stints in book design and ceramics. When it finally emerged it did so all of a piece—an intellectual entity, complete in itself. It had about it the air of finality of a natural structure. It stayed that way throughout a long career. With unwavering consistency of invention he produced poster after poster; he achieved the aim of every designer—recognisability without repetition. His was no formula-approach; each of his designs was a fresh beginning and a completely original statement. By the time the war came—just eight years after his first poster appeared—he was doyen of the nationally famous coterie of artists in the Munich group.

In the revolution that he brought about, Hohlwein was to his time as Cassandre and Kauffer were to theirs. He is among the immortals.

Like so many other artists, his war posters are at their best where they show the greatest conviction. Where they show compassion they are often even better. Hohlwein's 'humanitarian' posters (funds for the wounded, for prisoners of war, and for the Red Cross) are examples of the power of sincerity. In his poster appeal for the war-wounded [127] we see a milestone in the history of the Poster. Here, in an idiom of absolute reality, in an image of irreducible simplicity we have the full story of the problem of the returning wounded soldier. The dismay and uncertainty of the expression, the contrast of newly-acquired crutches with the tools of an almost-forgotten trade, the convalescent disarray, the loneliness of the figure as it stoops to take up life again—these tell a poster story of unusual complexity. It is not just the *Please help, I'm wounded* story of the usual appeal poster; it is a paragraph or two of reasoned statement and it spells it out with a maximum of emotional impact. That it does so with such an economy of word and image is a triumph of poster virtuosity.

Writing in 1920, an American poster pundit was to report: 'I have it upon first-hand information that nothing of any marked degree of merit appeared in Germany during the war. . . . If anything, the stress of war served chiefly to intensify and exaggerate that heavy quality, akin to brutality, that bids fair to characterise the German poster of post-war days. The war added no inspirational quality, no note of nobility or spiritual uplift to the German poster, and in many instances the poster was employed rather as a means of inspiring hatred of England than patriotic fervour for the fatherland.' The fog of war took a long time to lift.

In virtually every one of the belligerent countries the poster scene was marked by controversy. In both Britain and Germany there were protests that posters were too 'pretty-pretty'—or too horrific. There were protests from poster artists, whose expertise was ignored in favour of printers' 'draughtsmen'. In Germany, posters were condemned for 'bad artistic taste' and for 'bombast'. In Italy there were complaints that certain Red Cross posters were unduly 'pitiful'. ('We do not need to be reminded so forcibly of the nastiness of war. We know it. The symbol itself—the Red Cross—is enough to remind us of our need for charity.')

To escape the barrage of good advice that came from all directions at once, many authorities sought refuge in the poster competition—a device which was to become standard public-relations practice throughout the world. Whether it always produced the best posters for the job is an open question; certainly it had the side-effect of focusing the attention of large numbers of competitors—and often their families, friends, and relations—on the subject matter in hand. War poster exhibitions, prize givings, and similar public occasions brought additional publicity benefit; production and posting up of the winning entries, instead of going unheralded, became a matter of public attention and comment. For the extended period that the operation covered, the man-in-the-street was brought in as a consultant behind the publicity scenes. It is a role that the public is notoriously ready to play; to be privy to the conspiracy of its own persuasion is an honour that few will decline without at least a passing thought.

The poster competition proliferated everywhere. Sometimes it was open to the world at large, sometimes only to specific bits of it. Sometimes there was only the slenderest hope that any of the entries would reach a publishable standard. Often the competition was mounted for its side-effects alone.

In a tennis court in the gardens of the Tuileries in the summer of 1917 there was an exhibition of posters submitted in a competition among serving soldiers. Organised by the *Bulletin des Armées*, a weekly paper for the forces, and baited with prize money donated by two Army officers, the competition drew over 300 entries and large crowds to view them at the *Salon du Poilu* in the tennis court. The winners, Private Dangon and Ambulanceman Carrière, were just the winners.

In competitions among French schoolchildren and members of youth organisations, the winners' designs were reproduced and published. With the chance of a real-life part in the national propaganda effort, children were quick to enter. Taking her place among the Poulbots, the Brangwyns, the Hohlweins and the other immortals, 16-year-old Marthe Picard was the winner of one competition organised by the *Comité National de Prévoyance et d'Economies*. The message of her entry [238] was *Eat less meat. Conserve our livestock*. Said another published entry, *Save wine for our soldiers*. Another, a sugar-ration poster by a 15-year-old, said *Rationing gives us all a little—but we all get it*. If the slogans were sometimes better than the designs, it was because the slogans were often provided by the management.

In Germany the design competition was a well-established convention. It had been the custom for a long while to set up competitions for all sorts of items—trade marks, postage stamps, award certificates, as well as posters. The German Poster Society *(Verein der Plakatfreunde)* was the co-ordinating body for the majority of these and it was this organisation that looked after most of Germany's war poster competitions. Karl Sigrist's 'hawk and dove' war-loan poster [91] was the outcome of one of these; so was Ferdy Horrmeyer's wounded soldier [136] with the caption —*and what about YOUR duty?* (This, like some of the more niggling British efforts, was to become famous—and much disliked.)

Subjects for poster competitions were by no means always straightforward. Towards the end of the war, with increasingly acute shortages of materials of every kind, the collection of women's hair for use in industrial processes became a patriotic duty. It was needed, said the authorities in Germany, for things like driving belts and insulation pads. The Poster Society, in conjunction with the Red Cross, organised a competition for a poster to encourage women to give their hair to the nation.

Among the 500 or so entries—some of them from leading designers— very few managed to convey the story in what the organisers had described as 'unambiguous and palatable form'. There were comb-gleanings, wisps of hair, tangles of hair, hanks of hair and single hairs; there was hair used as bows for arrows, as driving belts—and as a variety of other obscure industrial gadgets. It had been anticipated that the subject was not without its hazards. Fears were well-founded. Lamenting the depths to which a number of competitors had been apparently obliged to dredge for their ideas, the Poster Society's report regretfully quoted a couplet devised by one competitor: *Die Rüstungsräde stehen still, wenns kein Härlein trieben will* (roughly: *The War Machine will come to a stop, without a hair-drive on the job*). It is clear that the war-poster competition, for competitors and judges alike, was by no means plain sailing.

Nor, even when the event was restricted to leading professionals, were the results always an unqualified success. In one such closed-shop operation for a soldiers' appeal poster, ten well-known designers were called in. Not one of them came up with anything more than mediocre. The organisers gave a prize to one and published his design. They gave a consolation prize to a 'runner-up'—and then commissioned Ludwig Hohlwein to do a really good one. As it turned out, they didn't like Hohlwein's either. It was agreed that the 15,000 marks that the whole operation had cost would have been better spent on something else.

In America the poster competition was put on a distinctly more economical footing by the elimination of the prize money. Throwing their assignments directly at art students, the authorities latched on to the creative zeal of enormous numbers of the country's poster hopefuls. The result was a tidal wave of ideas—none of them very good.

The Chicago Academy of Fine Arts reported that output was colossal. 'The Academy is making,' said its president, 'successful efforts to fit its training to the new war art needs of the country. One hundred and twenty-five large enlistment posters have already been made by the students. These were submitted for Government use, and those not reproduced were used by the students near their homes for the purpose for which they were designed.

'A group of food conservation posters has been sent to Washington which the committee referred to as the best they had seen. Seven have been chosen by the Government for national use.' (It must be noted in passing that in the production of these posters no effort had been spared to ensure success. The academics had provided everything that the students could need. To aid the designing of food conservation posters there were 'large piles of food to be conserved . . . as still-life subjects instead of the usual pottery and flowers'. There were also 'models appropriately costumed in uniform, employed by the school for the pupils' use'. And as a final contribution to the new war-art needs of the country 'large silk flags were kept in motion by electric fans while the students painted them in motion'. There was no doubt that the Chicago Academy of Fine Arts was now on a full-scale war footing.)

The president of the Academy told the press of the success of Chicago's Women's Registration Week, a scheme for the enlistment of female war workers. This too was grist to the mill of the Academy. 'The Week was used as another problem by the students,' said the president. 'Thirty-five posters were made for this patriotic duty.' Of these, one was chosen to be reproduced and posted throughout the city. Unfortunately it did not escape criticism; the Army was obliged to point out that although it said *Back him up*, which was good, it showed an American soldier moving into battle wearing the soft home-service uniform hat, which was bad.

It was later decided to assign military advisers to art school operations of this kind. The mistake became too frequent. But in fairness to the students it must be recorded that they were not alone in their error. No less an operator than Lucien Jonas, the distinguished French artist, made the same mistake in his guardian-angel poster *(Souscrivez pour la Victoire)* [29] in which thousands of doughboys move in on the enemy at the double —soft-hatted, every one.

It is recorded that the Academy's 34 remaining posters were sold by auction 'for the benefit of the cause'. It will be seen how little waste there was.

Nor were other academic centres in the United States idle. The New

York School of Fine and Applied Art had war-poster painting classes too. So had the fine Arts Division of the New York Teachers' College. The School of Art spent one whole week painting posters for the National Guard. Then they were asked to work for the regular army. Ten thousand of their posters were distributed throughout New York City. ('The Army officer who is now working with them sees that all military details are correct.')

Said Everett Henry, in charge of the Army poster operation, 'The Army wants to put out new posters every ten days. We are working hard to supply enough designs. It is our desire to see all the art schools of the country fall in line and do this work for the Government.' Poster productivity in the United States was higher than anywhere else in the world.

It was by no means only from students that America got her posters. In April 1917, Charles Dana Gibson—inventor, among other national images, of the Gibson Girl—called a meeting of every notable illustrator and designer within hailing distance. He formed a committee, later to be known as the Division of Pictorial Publicity, and offered its design services to Washington. Washington accepted. Thereafter, for the seventeen months of America's war, Gibson's Committee met once a week (first, history has it, in Keen's Chop House, and later at the Salmagundi Club).

At each meeting requests for posters from Government departments or from voluntary organisations were farmed out to individuals in the group. Each of these 'captains', as they called themselves, was responsible for getting the designer he deemed best fitted for the job to do a rough sketch for submission through the Committee to the 'client'.

On this slap-happy basis, with none of the participants accepting fees of any kind, and with rough sketches batting back and forth like shuttlecocks, the group pumped out a total of some 700 poster designs for over fifty individual agencies. It is perhaps not surprising in the circumstances that not all of them were good.

Similar to the Gibson set-up was that of Henry Reuterdahl, naval painter extraordinary. He, with his own coterie of volunteers, moved in on the Navy. Without benefit of weekly meetings they did the Navy's bidding— also without fee. On the Reuterdahl talent list was every distinguished name that Gibson had not thought of, and many that he had.

Some designs (significantly, those with strong female-content) were resoundingly successful. Perhaps the most powerful of all war posters, put out by the Boston Committee of Public Safety, had been published in June 1915—nearly two years before America's entry into the war. This was Fred Spear's *Lusitania* poster [159]. The sinking, claimed on the one hand as a justifiable act of interception of illicit war materials and on the other as a wholesale murder of women and children, had cost over a thousand civilian lives, 128 of them American. The poster, with a mother and child sinking through the water and the one word *ENLIST*, had a devastating impact. Like the occasion that produced it, it was unforgettable.

Still to come were the more easily forgettable female figures of *Gee, I wish I were a man* [32]—in which a girl in a sailor suit yearns to join the Navy, and A. E. Foringer's equally doubtful image of *The Greatest Mother in the World* [120]. (The Greatest Mother figure, nursing a baby soldier on a baby stretcher, was to be the subject of much post-war psychological analysis. At the time she was so successful as to be adopted by the Red Cross as an unofficial trade mark. Indeed, she was successful enough to be brought into service in identical form in World War II.)

Already geared up to an intensive poster recruiting campaign before the declaration of war, in April 1917 America went poster-wild. Montgomery Flagg's pre-war war poster, *Wake Up, America*, distributed far and wide by the Mayor's Committee of New York, came into its own. On 14 April, five days after the declaration, the New York City Women's Suffrage Party, aided by an army of Boy Scouts, plastered the town with 20,000 recruiting posters. Five thousand posters appeared in the windows of the shops on Fifth Avenue and the New York Press Club held a show of British war posters. The Student's Fellowship of Chicago's Art Institute declared itself a 25,000-strong (poster) army, 'trained to render its country a kind of service to be given by no other body....' Posters and cartoons were a vital national need, they said, to bring before people the truth and to make them join the Army.

On the quagmire of the Western Front, now in its third year, losses on all sides had mounted beyond control. British losses had reached a steady 100,000 a month—noticeably more than the official War Office quota. For the single 24-hour period of 16 April 1917 the French Government estimated its losses in dead, wounded, prisoners of war and 'missing' as 150,000 men. German figures were well on the way to their final total of 7 million. The war was no longer an event; it was a condition. It was moving now towards the convulsions of Passchendaele, Cambrai, and the Marne. There was mass exhaustion.

Men were openly beginning to question the validity of it all. In at least sixteen corps of the French Army there was mutiny. There was mutiny in the German forces too. 'What we have done,' wrote Maurice Genevoix, in a famous phrase, 'what we have done was more than you can ask of men. And we did it.' In the spring of 1917 soldiers on all sides were losing the will to do it any more.

As the flags stirred in the breeze of the electric fans at the Chicago Academy of Fine Arts, the destruction lines in Europe awaited their American quota. Said one American poster artist, 'The game of war has

its horrible side, but it is not advisable to look upon that side in a poster. . . .'
He showed a fine grasp of the situation.

As a general rule, all of the war posters of all of the belligerents ignored the horrible side. There were notable—and sometimes surprising—incitements to actual violence (like Brangwyn's *Final Blow*, and the 'before' and 'after' pictures [192] of the effects of trench bombardment) but for the most part there was a careful avoidance of any suggestion that actual physical injury was inflicted on actual people. If violence, or its results, were depicted at all, it was invariably the violence of the enemy.

Diffidence about the actual details of war was a universal poster characteristic. When posters did boil over into graphic action there was a tendency for the enemy to be too far away to be distinguishable, or to be looking the other way, or to be hazy, or in shadow. More often than not he was off the edge of the poster altogether. In the rare cases where he was shown in detail he tended to be stupid, clumsy, dismayed, ugly—but never dead. A symbolic helmet lying in the dust was the closest that the poster got; with wholesale carnage at the battlefronts, with death and mutilation a round-the-clock occurrence for the eyes of millions in the trenches, at home there was a universal observance of the delicacies. Even at the height of mutual hatred, when the normal compassions had virtually disappeared, it still seemed not quite right to show the enemy actually dying. Killing people, when you got down to pictures of it—even if it was the enemy, even if only on posters—was somehow wrong.

As substitutes for killing, the poster resorted to a variety of less lasting punishments. There was a wide range of symbolic belabourings, of hammerings, crushings and poundings. But even some of these were criticised as being 'not quite the thing'. A British national service poster quoted a House of Commons speech by Mr Neville Chamberlain: *Germany means to starve us out. There is only one answer—a blow straight between the eyes.* The illustration showed an old-fashioned civilian right-arm jab, the shirt-sleeved contestants slugging it out in the tradition of the street corner. When the poster filtered through to Berlin, the comment was, 'Unconcealed brutality'. At least one Briton said that he found it 'somewhat surprising'. He thought it remarkable that 'such a violent pictorial illustration' should be permitted by a government department. 'I should have supposed,' he said, 'that it would have been considered much too undignified to be in any way associated with official advertising.'

On all sides, whatever the brutality levels of the war itself, there was a continual invocation of the dignities.

It was perhaps in the posters of Austria and Italy that this demanding sense of dignity was most prominent. Austria's allegorical figures and heraldics, her laurelled swords and battle-standards, were notable for their unbending knightliness. Only rarely did she break into the more general parlance of the wartime poster. (Even in that most bellicose of all war posters [185]—in which, under the title of *Our Pride* she celebrates her 30.5 cm shell—the heraldic note still sounds. United portraits of Franz-Joseph and William, a cast-iron double-headed eagle, and a complete calendar for the year 1915 contribute to an irreproachable respectability. The extended display-life conferred upon the design by the calendar is not to be sniffed at either; as well as being dignified, this poster is useful.)

In Italy the need for dignity was even more marked. Mauzan and Borgoni caught exactly the 'grand manner' that pervaded most of Italy's official wartime image.

With the female element never entirely absent, the Italian war poster combined a note of sex-appeal with a stateliness that was candidly out of this world. There is a continuing motif of the dominant female figure, solemnising allegiance, signposting the way to the battle, personally leading the soldiery into the front lines—and even, as in her allegorical encounter with Capranesi's astonished Ostrogoth [37]—going on active service herself.

Here again, only rarely is there incitement to any identifiable form of violence; when it does appear, as in Finozzi's *Drive them out* poster [41], it is a woman that does the inciting (and, characteristically, the enemy is well beyond the margins of the picture).

An important exception to the dominant-female formula—but not to that of the dignities of war—was Mauzan's dominant soldier: *Everyone to his duty!* [10] This was to take its place in the ranks of the world's army of exhortation—the pointing, beckoning, declaiming figures that called from everywhere to everyone for more of everything. No less compelling than his counterparts, the Italian version certainly appeared in greater numbers, and in a wider variety of shapes and sizes than the pointers and beckoners of any other country. He was hung in gigantic reproductions across the streets, posted in multiple sets on outsize hoardings, printed by the million as postcards, folders and leaflets, and reproduced in magazine and newspaper advertisements. Like Kitchener, he was also parodied. In political cartoons, in joke drawings and even in commercial advertising, new—and sometimes irreverent—versions of the figure appeared. It was an indignity that he survived: his accusing hand remained for decades, rankling in the general memory.

There was another indignity—in another poster—that only just survived. This was the famous *Sniper* poster. It was in the name of elegance alone that many citizens protested at the poster figure of a marksman perched on a battlefield tree stump. His ungainly posture, with his rear as notable a backward feature as the forward thrust of his rifle, was deemed to be unbecoming to a hero. Whatever might be the realities of war, said the civilian, let us at all costs not have realities that look ridiculous.

In the avoidance of disgrace, whether of foolishness at one end of the scale or, at the other end, of being shown actually killing people, much time and attention was spent by all concerned. For all of the belligerents the common denominator was self-respect. There were differences in visual temperament, differences of poster accent, but among the many points of agreement was the proposition that you must look neither cruel nor foolish.

If the posters of Italy abounded in the female figure, so did the French—perhaps even more so. But whereas with the Italians the keynote was a classic stateliness, with the French there was a vibrant sincerity, an urgent driving *panache* that carried the day with its own emotional integrity. Here too—as with Germany and Greece—there was no lack of guardian-angel war loan salesmanship, no shortage of female exhortation. Like the figures of Britannia, Germania and Italia (not to mention sundry other national females), Marianne of France was on instant call throughout the war. But where Britannia posed and Italia postured, Marianne weighed in without reserve. Thomas Fasche's double-eagle-chested lady for the Austrian War Loan [35], so similar in basic concept to the Georges Scott lady for the Emprunt National [36], is a case in point. Where the one is cool, decent, and considered, the other has the fire and fury of true inspiration. The girl from Vienna is calmly mute; she wears sensible clothes and a pleasant smile. Marianne is rough, tough, and real; her clothes are in attractive disarray and she is bawling her head off. In the juxtaposition of these two drawings we see the whole story of the difference between France and all the rest; almost without exception, France's posters have a vigour and emotional impact that raise them far above their counterparts. With this air of unselfconscious spontaneity, the inherent unbelievability of the subject is made almost credible. The Austrian girl, we feel, did not exist; Marianne maybe did.

We see the same characteristic in a comparison of approaches to the 'guardian angel' theme—particularly in the juxtaposition of Stieborsky's Austrian War Loan angel [28] and that of Lucien Jonas [29] for the Emprunt National. Where the Austrian version has an air of deadpan contrivedness, the French rendering, for all its airy-fairy allegory, has conviction and abounding life. Even with all those Americans in soft hats, even with the levitating lady, we come close to a suspension of disbelief.

(It must be recorded in connection with the Jonas poster that the hovering angel, accoutred as she is with the sword, laurels, and near-nakedness of her office, was perhaps considered to be not quite lively enough. The poster exists in another version in which, instead of placidly surveying the grenade-throwing *poilu*, she turns her head to look in the direction of the enemy. The rest of the poster, although entirely redrawn, is unchanged except for the addition of traces of shrapnel from an explosion in the middle distance—and an open-mouthed yell from the lady. It would seem that the poster was the subject of discussion; it exists in no fewer than four distinct renderings. History is uncertain not only as to the reason for the changes, but indeed as to their sequence. It is even possible that the angel was felt, on the contrary, to be too lively—and that the placid version was the final one. But whichever version we settle for as 'official', the force of the contrast with the woodenness of its Austrian counterpart remains.)

If national characteristics provided refreshing differences of style, they did nothing to disturb the universality of the general pattern. Not only in the sequence of its phases, but in the detail of its psychology, each country's poster programme observed the international rules. And it was not just in the matter of pictorial presentation that it conformed; in its slogans too there was close identity.

Top of the official list of psychological pressures (but by no means the most effective) is the appeal to the sense of duty. *My duty!* says the British paterfamilias [55] as he digs into his pocket for a War Loan contribution; *Your duty, buy US Government Bonds*, says America [172] to its new immigrants. *Eux aussi, font leurs devoir (They too are doing their duty)* says a wounded *poilu* as he watches honest citizens buying their bonds. *Und eure Pflicht? (And YOUR duty?)*—says Ferdy Horrmeyer's wounded soldier from beneath his bandages. *Fate tutti il vostro dovere! (Everyone to his duty!)* calls Italy's Kitchener-figure [10]. *Bauern, tut euere Pflicht; die Städte hungern! (Farmers, do your duty; the towns are hungry!)* says the weeping Hönich family [158]. *Do your duty to our boys as they are doing theirs to you* says Brangwyn in his poster for the War Society [112].

Duty gets a big airing in war. So does religion. *God save the King*, says the Zeppelin poster [15]. *Herrgott, erhalte uns die Kärntner-Heimat (Dear God, preserve our Karinthian homeland)*; *Thank God and the sailors for my good breakfast*; *Gibst Du ein Scherklein noch so klein, in Gott soll Dir's gesegnet sein (However small the mite you give, God will bless you, long as you live)*; *God speed the plough and the woman who drives it* [237]; *Gott befohlen! Ihr Lieber zuhaus, hoffet und betet, wir harren aus (God be with you. Your loved ones at home await you)* [104]; *God bless Daddy who is fighting the Hun—and send him help!*

The saints also served. At least one, St George, joined God in doing double duty—on one side for British recruitment [64] and on the other [65] for the Sixth Austrian War Loan.

As we have seen, it was a function of war persuasion to shame the civilian with the sacrifices of the soldier. This was a specially productive field: *Er trägt das Kreuz für uns; Was tun wir gleiches? (He carries the cross for us; what are WE doing?); Essi rischiano tutto . . . Sottoscrivete! (They risk everything . . . Subscribe!); Es sage Niemand, 'Ich habe schon gegeben'; unsere Truppen sagen auch nicht, 'Wir haben schon gekämpft' (Let no one say, 'I have already given'; our troops do not say, 'We have already fought'* [76]*);* Shall we be more tender with our dollars than with the lives of our men? [57]; *Ich gehe hinaus an die Front; hast Du schon die Kriegsanleihe gezeichnet? (I am off to the front; have you bought a War Loan?* [9]*)*.

In even sharper terms there was shaming by casualty: *Dies tat Ich für Dich* [133], says a wounded soldier, *'Was tust Du für mich?' (I did this for you; what are you doing for me?).* Says an amputee [134], *Ed ora a Voi! (Now it's your turn!).* Says a nurse as she escorts a blinded soldier [135], *What are you doing to help?* And, mincing no words, another blinded soldier says [132], *Per la patria, i miei occhi; per la pace il vostro denaro! (For the country, my eyes; for peace, your money.)* With a final tug at the purse [138] there are the white faces of children: *Nostro padre ha dato la vita; voi non negherete il denaro . . . (Our father gave his life; you will not deny your money?).*

But beating the civilian with the stick of shame cannot go on indefinitely. There has to be the carrot of promise. Here the formula is to translate the war effort into an effort for peace [195]: *Durch Sieg zum Frieden (Through Victory to Peace).* The proposition is summed up neatly—in this case without the use of words at all—in Karl Sigrist's neck-and-neck rendering of hawk and dove [91] in his prize-winning War Loan poster. There comes a stage when military victory is presented not, as was the case initially, as an end in itself, but as a synonym for the peace that has been gone so long—the key to a return to the good times. *Bringt Euer Geld,* says a little mother [220], *helft zum Frieden—und das Glück kommt wieder! (Bring your money; help towards peace—and happiness again!)* In the same vein an Italian slogan: *Date denaro per la vittoria—la vittoria e pace (Give money for victory—victory and peace).*

Sometimes it is a more personal form of peace that is offered. As a woman waits with her children for her absent husband [145] a slogan says, *Per ritorno vittorioso, sottoscrivete al prestito (For a victorious return, subscribe to the loan!)* In Austria too: *Je mehr der Mittel zur kraftvollen Wehr, um so früher die Wiederkehr (The stronger the army, the quicker the return).* A less ambitious promise was conveyed in Poulbot's child collectors for the 1915 *Journée du Poilu* [47]—*Pour que Papa vienne en permission, s'il vous plaît (So that Daddy can come home on leave, please).*

In more desperate mood, but with not too obviously ambiguous overtones, is the classic call for a last effort. As Allied soldiers climb to dislodge an eagle from its eyrie, the slogan says *Un dernier effort, et on l'aura! (One last effort and we'll have him!)* A latter-day Siegfried [63] takes aim for a final hack at the head of a lion: *Es gilt die letzten Schläge, den Sieg zu vollenden (It takes the last blows to bring victory).*

A French general looks at us over his shoulder as battle-stained troops march by: *Pour le dernier quart d'heure . . . aidez-moi! (For the last quarter of an hour . . . help me!).* In an Austrian poster civilians are shown helping to complete the bridge of victory as Peace waits in her chariot to cross over it: *Helft mit den Schlußstein legen! (Help to lay the last stone).* And Frank Brangwyn RA [67] bayonets his already-reeling German soldier: *Put strength in the final blow.*

In the universality of the general pattern there were similarities of detail, not only in slogans and poster images, not only in the psychology of direct persuasion, but in peripheral details. Less directly related to the prosecution of the war—even if it did contain some promise of peace—was the matter of the commemoration of the dead. We see that in the summer of 1916, on both sides, the time had officially come to consider this. In Leipzig and in London, within scarcely three weeks of each other, there were exhibitions of designs for war memorials [154, 155]. As it turned out there were still some years, and many millions more men, to go.

As we observe the similarities that pervade the posters of the 1914–18 war, the feeling grows that here was unanimity amounting almost to conspiracy. Or was it plagiarism? Or just coincidence?

Plagiarism there undoubtedly was. The Greek rendering of Leroux's family parting [44, 45] is a straight lift. So, certainly, was the Canadian version of *Women of Britain say GO!*—rendered (without undue creative zeal) as *Women of Canada say GO!* So was the disastrous adaptation of Whistler's mother, filched, with the addition of *Old Age Must Come,* by the British War Savings Campaign from the *Fight for Her* version of the Irish Canadian Rangers. Where firing lines did not intervene there was a brisk turnover in breach of copyright.

But there are similarities and parallels that owe nothing to mere cribbing. They are designers' solutions, in almost identical terms, of almost identical problems. It is in the highest degree unlikely that Dudovich in Italy [114] stole his Red Cross design from Richard Klein's Red Cross design [113] in Germany, or that Joyce Dennys with her British appeal for nurses [122] stole from either. The red cross, that serves in each case as a backdrop to the figures, is a logical design element; so are the figures. The similarity of treatment should not really come as a surprise.

On reflection it must be conceded that, as between belligerents on opposing sides, points of poster identity are no more coincidental—and certainly no more to be wondered at—than the fact that all of the belligerents used

armies to fight with.   If there was not a great deal to choose between the
bullets fired by one side or the other, if men on both sides had uniforms
and letters from home and shell-shock and lice, if the disciplines of battle
were much the same whichever army you were in—it is little wonder
that posters and the other trimmings were much the same as well.
Posters, like every other element in the situation, were part of the universal
trap.   They complement each other, fitting together like the parts of an
interlocking puzzle.   When we see them side by side, often as mirror
images of each other, we see them as a total system, a simple system of
destruction.

Above all we see the presence of universal archetypes: the square-
jawed handsome hero, the compassionate nurse, the weeping refugee.
They are the timeless persons of the drama; we are their understudies.
Whatever his nationality, the soldier—if he is 'ours'—has always the same
nobility of bearing, the same immediately likable, thoroughly decent air
of right and might.   And so with the rest of them; decency, compassion,
nobility and righteousness abound.   Not one of us—not one of 'ours', at
least—is ugly, stupid, nasty, or wrong.

It is in this universal dedication to the upright and honest that the heart
of the matter lies.

It is at once the most hopeful—and ironically the most tragic of human
characteristics; it is the fuel-cell of peace—and the power-house of war.

INDEX OF ARTISTS

Scott, Septimus E: 189
Scrivener, W H: 196
Smet, Leon de: 125
Spencer Pryse, G: 18, 117
Stewart, Allen: 20
T E: 87
U J B: 225
Van Dusen, Howard: 179
Welsh: 197

GREECE

Anon: 1, 27, 31, 69, 83, 98, 107, 131, 213
'Geo': 45

HUNGARY

Anon: 110
Biro: 53, 146
Kádor: 153
Kober, Leo: 59
Rubes: 81
Weiss, Antal: 75

ITALY

Anon: 34, 145
Barchi: 7, 103
Bonzagni, A: 134
Borgoni, M: 30, 82
Caffonaro: 187
Capranesi, G: 37
Dudovich, M: 114
Finozzi, Ugo: 41
Mauzan: 10, 26
Ortelli, A: 132
Varino: 177
Vinca, M: 138

POLAND

Anon: 108

RUSSIA

Anon: 86, 95, 102, 191
Butschkin, T: 84

Kustodieff, B: 71
Tsheltsov, E: 8
Varmanski, V: 186

SOUTH AFRICA

Anon: 19

UNITED STATES OF AMERICA

Anon: 49, 137, 162, 166, 169, 170, 171, 172, 176, 240
Babcock: 161
Bancroft, Milton: 118
Britton, L N: 173, 224
Bull, Charles Livingstone: 94
Christy, Howard: 32, 160
Coughlin, John A: 165
Dewey: 48
Dunne, Harvey: 231
Falls, C B: 200
Flagg, James Montgomery: 3, 14, 57
Foringer, A E: 120
Grant, Gordon: 135
Kiek, Rev. S A: 119
Leyendecker, J C: 50
Maris, Walter de: 143
McCoy, Arthur G: 119
Morgan, Wallace: 233
Norton, John: 174
Paus: 188
Penfield, Edward: 235
Pennell, Joseph: 61
Preissig, Vogtech: 78, 109
Raleigh: 175, 227
Rogers, W A: 180
Shafer, L A: 167
Spear, Fred: 159
Sterner, Albert: 121
Strothman, F: 184
Taylor, Walter: 168
Triedler, Adolph: 194
Whitehead, Walter: 73
Williams, J Scott: 33
Young, Crawford: 228
Young, Ellsworth: 182

ACKNOWLEDGEMENTS

Among the many organizations and individuals who have helped in the preparation of this book, the author and publisher would especially like to thank the Keeper of the Department of Printed Books of the British Museum, London; the Director and staff of the Library and of the Department of Exhibits of the Imperial War Museum, London; the Director and staff of the Print Department of the Victoria and Albert Museum, London; the Conservateur en Chef of the Musée de la Guerre, Paris; the Library of the Institut Français du Royaume-Uni, London; the Library of the German Institute, London; the United States Library, University of London; the Library of the Advertising Association, London; the Library of the St Bride Foundation Institute, London; and the Library Services of the City of Westminster.

2 BRITAIN

John Hassall

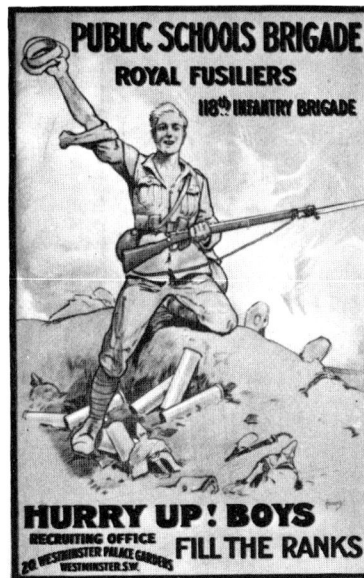

1 GREECE

Anonymous

Greeks! Arise! / Barbarians are killing our brothers, burning our villages ... To arms!

3 USA

James Montgomery Flagg

4 BRITAIN

Frank Brangwyn

5 FRANCE
Jules Abel Faivre
We will get them! /
Subscribe to the Second
National Defence Loan

"YOUR COUNTRY NEEDS YOU"

6 BRITAIN
Alfred Leete

7 ITALY

Barchi

Help us to win! / Subscribe to 5% Consolidated Stock

8 RUSSIA

E. Tsheltsov

Subscribe to the 5½% War Loan / More money means more munitions!

9 AUSTRIA

Magda Koll

I am off to the front. Have you bought your War Loan?

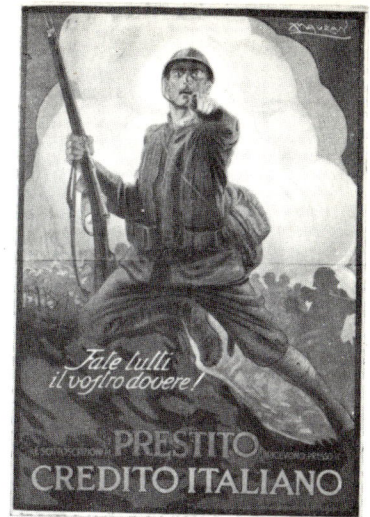

10 ITALY

Mauzan

Everyone to his duty! / Loan subscriptions are received at Credito Italiano

14 USA

James Montgomery Flagg

11 BRITAIN

Anonymous

12 BRITAIN

Anonymous

13 BRITAIN

Anonymous

16 AUSTRALIA
Norman Lindsay

Fall-in!

ISSUED BY THE GOVERNMENT OF THE COMMONWEALTH OF AUSTRALIA   W. E. SMITH LTD. SYDNEY

IT IS FAR BETTER
TO FACE THE BULLETS
THAN TO BE KILLED
AT HOME BY A BOMB

JOIN THE ARMY AT ONCE
& HELP TO STOP AN AIR RAID

GOD SAVE THE KING

15 BRITAIN
Anonymous

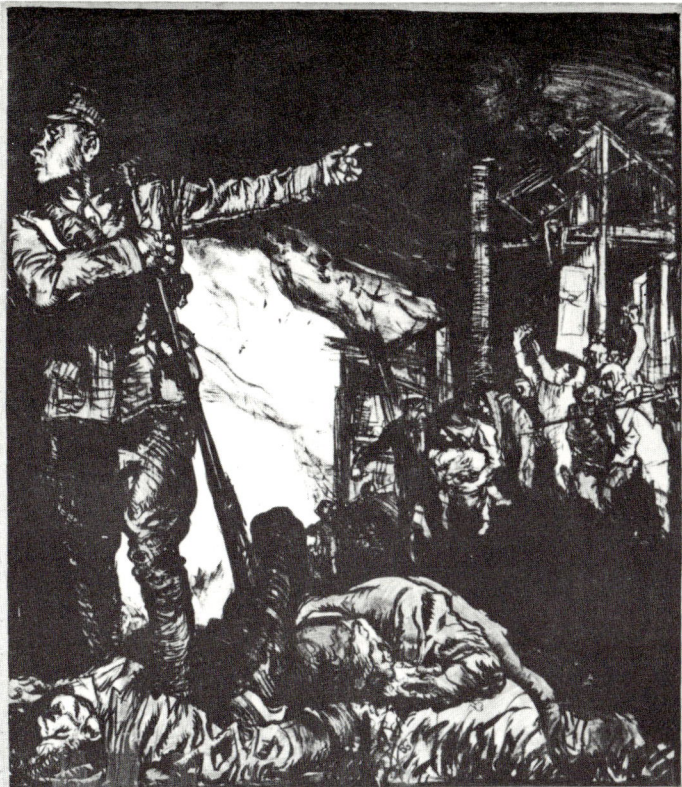

WAR
TO ARMS CITIZENS
OF THE EMPIRE!!

17 BRITAIN
Frank Brangwyn

Through Darkness to Light THE ONLY ROAD FOR AN ENGLISHMAN *Through Fighting to Triumph*

18 BRITAIN
G. Spencer Pryse

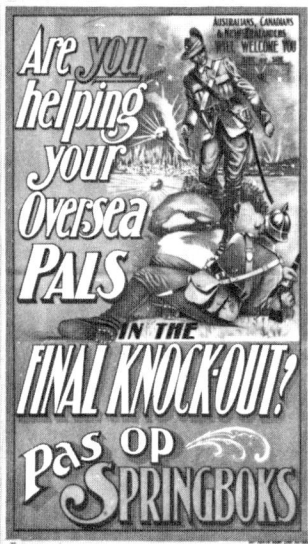

19 SOUTH AFRICA
Anonymous

· COME AND HELP US ·

· FOR HONOUR · FOR FREEDOM ·

20 BRITAIN
Allen Stewart

BRITAIN'S NEW
MILLION ARMY

COMPLETE THE
SECOND HALF-MILLION

Men wishing
to Join Fall
in and Follow
the Band

21 BRITAIN

G. R.

FOR THOSE WHO WANT TO
SERVE THEIR COUNTRY

Men who are medically fit,
who are 5 ft. 3 ins. high and upwards,
whose chest measurement is at least 34 ins.
can join the Army under the following conditions:
either
FOR THE DURATION OF THE WAR
In this case the age limits are:
if ex-regular Soldiers, 19–42 years,
other men - - - 19–30 „
or
for the following periods, according to the arm which they join:

| CAVALRY INFANTRY A.S.C. | 7 years with the colours, 5 in the reserve. |
| R.H. & R.F.A., R.E. | 6 years with the colours, 6 in the reserve. |

AGE 18–25.
Apply at any Military Barrack or Recruiting Office. The address of nearest Recruiter
can be ascertained at any Post Office or Labour Exchange.

GOD SAVE THE KING

22 BRITAIN

REMEMBER BELGIUM

ENLIST TO-DAY

24 BRITAIN
Anonymous

"A Happy New Year
to our Gallant Soldiers!"

VICTORY

1915

You can
Make it certain
if you

JOIN NOW

25 BRITAIN
Anonymous

TO THE
YOUNG WOMEN
OF LONDON

Is your "Best Boy" wearing
Khaki? If not don't YOU
THINK he should be?

If he does not think that you
and your country are worth
fighting for—do you think he
is WORTHY of you?

Don't pity the girl who is
alone—her young man is
probably a soldier—fighting
for her and her country—
and for YOU.

If your young man neglects his duty to his
King and Country, the time may come when
he will NEGLECT YOU.

Think it over—then ask him to

JOIN THE ARMY TO-DAY

23 BRITAIN

26 ITALY
Mauzan
" ... and what was ours is ours again ". / Liberation Loan
(The reference is to territories incorporated
in the Austro-Hungarian Empire)

27 GREECE
Anonymous
Investment Bonds / available at every bank

30 ITALY

M. Borgoni
National Loan

31 GREECE

Anonymous
Ask for the Investment Bond / 4½% and 5%

28 AUSTRIA
Willy Stieborsky
Subscribe to the Sixth Austrian War Loan

29 FRANCE
Lucien Jonas
Subscribe for Victory — and for the Triumph of Freedom

32 USA
Howard Chandler

33 USA
J. Scott Williams

34 ITALY
(.....?)
Ever onward!

35 AUSTRIA

Thomas Fasche
Subscribe to the Seventh War Loan

36 FRANCE

Georges Scott
*For the Flag! For Victory /
Subscribe to the
National Loan*

*Pour le Drapeau!
Pour la Victoire!*

SOUSCRIVEZ à L'EMPRUNT NATIONAL
LES SOUSCRIPTIONS SONT REÇUES A PARIS ET EN PROVINCE
À LA
BANQUE NATIONALE DE CRÉDIT

DEVAMBEZ. IMP. PARIS

VISA N° 9.498

SOTTOSCRIVETE AL PRESTITO

G. Capranesi

37 ITALY
G. Capranesi
National Loan

38 AUSTRIA
A.S.
Subscribe to the Fifth War Loan

39 BRITAIN
Anonymous

40 BRITAIN
E. V. Kealey

41 ITALY
Ugo Finozzi
Drive them out!

Altona's
Opfertag
18. Januar 1916

Altonaer! Am Tage der Reichsgründung gedenket derer, die durch den großen Kampf um des Reiches Bestand in Not geraten sind. Schafft neue Mittel für die Altonaer Kriegshilfe

Kunstanstalt Langebartels & Jürgens Altona

42 GERMANY

W. Gallerman
Altona's Gift Day
(War Relief Appea

46 BRITAIN
Savile Lumley

Daddy, what did YOU do in the Great War?

44 FRANCE

Auguste Leroux
For fighting France!
For the one that
grows every day

43 AUSTRIA

K. Stedder

3ᵉ EMPRUNT
DE LA DÉFENSE NATIONALE
Souscrivez

pour la France qui combat !
pour Celle qui chaque jour grandit.

ΕΝΤΟΚΑ ΤΑΜΕΙΑΚΑ ΓΡΑΜΜΑΤΙΑ
ΖΗΤΗΣΑΤΕ ΕΙΣ ΤΑΣ ΤΡΑΠΕΖΑΣ

Γιά τήν Ἑλλάδα πού πολεμᾶ
καὶ γιά τὸ μέλλον τῶν παιδιῶν σας

45 GREECE

" Geo "

Investment Bonds /
Ask at the bank /
For Greece that fights
for your children's future

JOURNÉE DU POILU

Pour que papa vienne en permission, s'il vous plaît.

25 ET 26
DÉCEMBRE
1915

ORGANISÉE PAR LE PARLEMENT

DEVAMBEZ Imp. PARIS

Our Deddy is fighting
at the Front for You—
Back him up— Buy a
United States Gov't Bond of the
2nd LIBERTY LOAN
of 1917

48 USA
Dewey

47 FRANCE

Francisque Poulbot
*Soldier's Day /
So that daddy will be
able to come
home on leave, please*

U★S★A BONDS

Third
Liberty Loan
Campaign
BOY SCOUTS
OF AMERICA

Be prepared

WEAPONS FOR LIBERTY

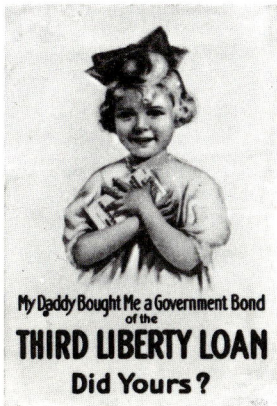

My Daddy Bought Me a Government Bond
of the
THIRD LIBERTY LOAN
Did Yours?

51 AUSTRIA
Alfred Offner
Subscribe to the Seventh War Loan

55 BRITAIN
E. V. Kealey

56 AUSTRIA
Alfred Offner
*Subscribe to
the Eighth War Loan*

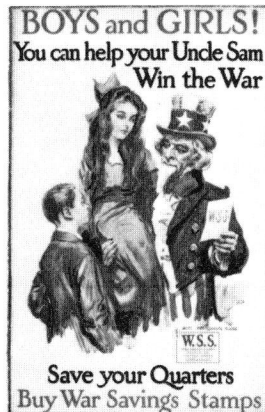

57 USA
James Montgomery Flagg

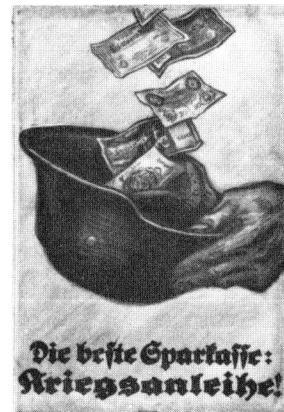

58 GERMANY
Louis Oppenheim
*The Best Savings Bank
- War Loan!*

52 FRANCE

Jules Abel Faivre

*Pour out your gold for France /
Gold fights for Victory*

53 HUNGARY

Biró

Money helps towards Victory - Subscribe!

54 AUSTRIA

Moldovany

*Help us in the struggle for
peace! / Subscribe to
War Loan*

59 HUNGARY

Leó Kober

Take out War Loan Insurance

60 GERMANY

Anonymous

*Lots of little makes
a lot / many minutes make
an hour; / that is why we all
must give / many givings give
us power!*

IOSEPH PENNELL DEL.

THAT LIBERTY SHALL NOT
PERISH FROM THE EARTH
BUY LIBERTY BONDS
FOURTH LIBERTY LOAN

61 USA
Joseph Pennell

Zeichnet die
6. Kriegsanleihe!
Centralbank der deutschen Sparkassen

249

Es gilt die letzten Schläge,
den Sieg zu vollenden!

Zeichnet
Kriegsanleihe!

63 GERMANY
Paul Gerd
*Now — the last blow for
final victory /
Subscribe to
the War Loan*

64 AUSTRIA

M. Lenz
the Sixth War Loan!
Subscribe to

65 BRITAIN

Anonymous

66 FRANCE
Lucien Jonas
Buy Liberation Loan

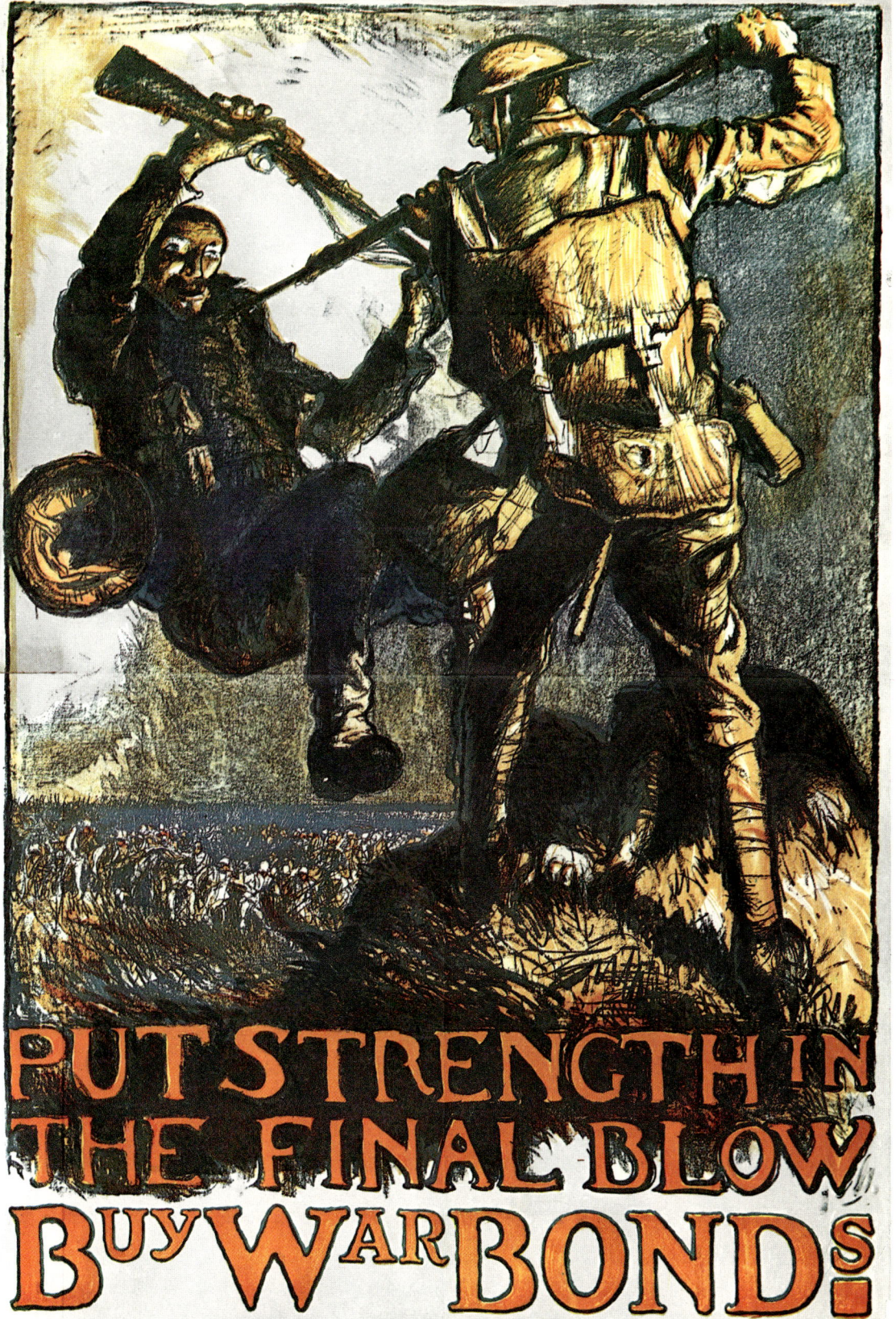

PUT STRENGTH IN THE FINAL BLOW
BUY WAR BONDS

ON NE 1914 PASSE PAS! 1918

Par deux fois j'ai tenu et vaincu sur la Marne,
Civil, mon frère,
la sournoise offensive de la "paix blanché va t'assaillira ton tour,
Comme moi, tu dois tenir et vaincre, sois fort et malin.
Méfie-toi de l'hypocrisie boche.

Union des Grandes Associations Françaises contre la propagande ennemie.

68 FRANCE

Maurice Neumon
*They do not pass! / Twice I have stood and conquered
on the Marne. Brother civilian, the cunning " peace
offensive " starts on you; like me, you must stand and win.
Be strong; be shrewd. Beware of Boche hypocrisy.*

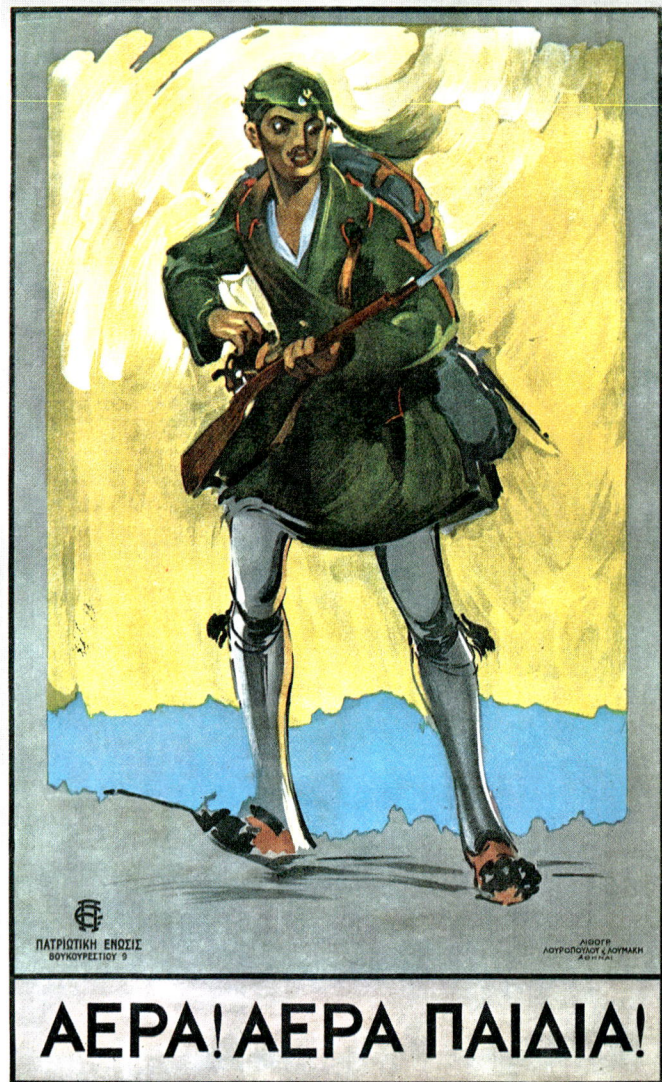

ΠΑΤΡΙΩΤΙΚΗ ΕΝΩΣΙΣ
ΒΟΥΚΟΥΡΕΣΤΙΟΥ 9

ΛΙΘΟΓΡ
ΛΟΥΡΟΠΟΥΛΟΥ & ΛΟΥΜΑΚΗ
ΑΘΗΝΑΙ

ΑΕΡΑ! ΑΕΡΑ ΠΑΙΔΙΑ!

69 GREECE

Anonymou
Freedom, lads

70 GERMANY

Hans Friedrich

Through our Army — the Freedom of the Seas!

71 RUSSIA

B. Kustodieff

Freedom Loan

72 AUSTRIA
W. Kuhn
Subscribe to the Sixth War Loan

73 USA
Walter Whitehead

74 AUSTRIA
Sterrer
Subscribe to War Loan

75 HUNGARY
Antal Weiss
Subscribe to the War Loan!

76 GERMANY
O. Weil
Hamburg Gift Day / No-one says " I have
already given " — nor do our troops say
" We have already fought ". / Hamburg's Army
and Navy Gift Day

77 AUSTRIA
A.S.P.
Soldiers' Welfare Week

78 *US* / (Czechoslovak Recruiting Office)
Vogtech Preissig

81 HUNGARY
Rubes
Subscribe to
the 6th Hungarian War Loan

79 GERMANY
Otto Leonard
Back up our troops /
Bring down England /
Buy War bonds

82 ITALY
M. Borgoni
National Loan

80 FRANCE
Jules Abel Faivre
3rd National Defence Loan; Subscribe!

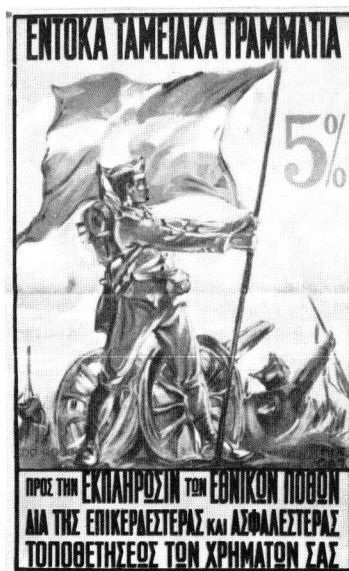

83 GREECE
Anonymous
5% Investment Bonds /
For achieving
the national aims; for investme
- with security and interest

T. Butschkin
*Freedom Loan /
War till Victory!*

FORWARD!

Forward to Victory
ENLIST NOW

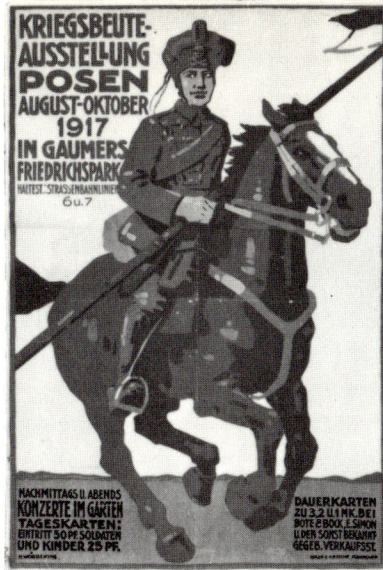

88 GERMANY
H. Wöbbeking
War Trophies Exhibition, Posen

89 FRANCE
D. Charles Fouqueray
African and Colonial Army Day

86 RUSSIA
Anonymous
*Subscribe to the
5½% War Loan and help our
valiant soldiers to Victory!*

87 BRITAIN
T.E.

SOVSCRIVEZ AV 4.ᵉ EMPRVN

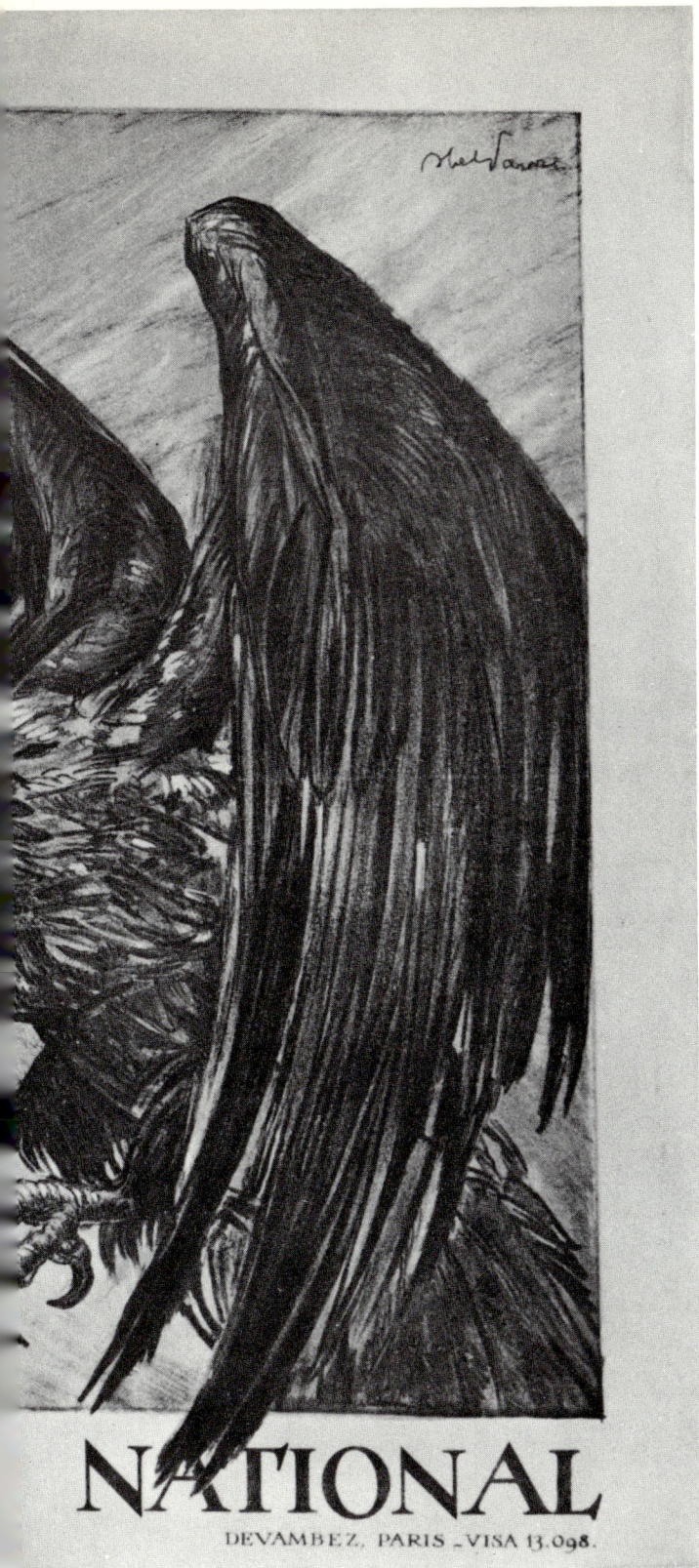

NATIONAL

DEVAMBEZ, PARIS _ VISA 13.098.

90 FRANCE
Jules Abel Faivre
*Subscribe to
the 4th National Loan*

Zeichnet Kriegsanleihe

91 GERMANY
Karl Sigrist
War Loan

Pour le suprême Effort

EMPRUNT NATIONAL
SOCIÉTÉ GÉNÉRALE

92 FRANCE
M. Falter
*For the Supreme Effort ... /
National Loan*

ZEICHNET
DIE KRIEGS-
ANLEIHE

Sie bringt den Frieden näher

93 GERMANY
F. Brantzky
War Loan — hastens Peace

KEEP HIM FREE

BUY W.S.S.
WAR SAVINGS STAMPS
ISSUED BY THE UNITED STATES TREASURY DEPT.

94 USA
Charles Livingstone Bull

Подпишитесь на
Военный
5½% заемъ
проложите путь
къ побѣдѣ

95 RUSSIA

(.....?)

Subscribe to
the 5½% War Loan
— and pave the way
to Victory!

96 GERMANY

Max Mandl
Just a little longer
(Exhibition of Air War Trophies)

97 GERMANY

Julius Gipkens
Air War Trophies Exhibition

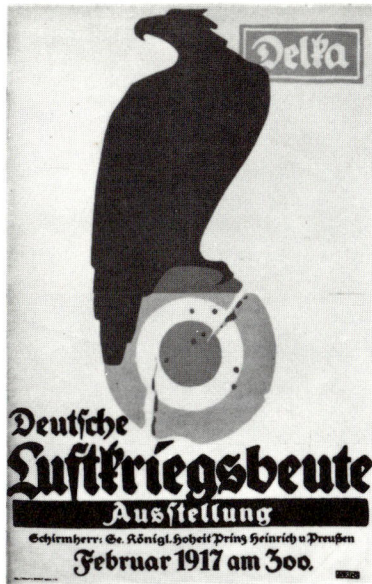

99 GERMANY

Julius Gipkens
*Help our heroic airmen
and their dependants*

98 GREECE

*Hambas bombing the " Geben " /
Hambas died 7 January 1918 /
Honour and Glory*

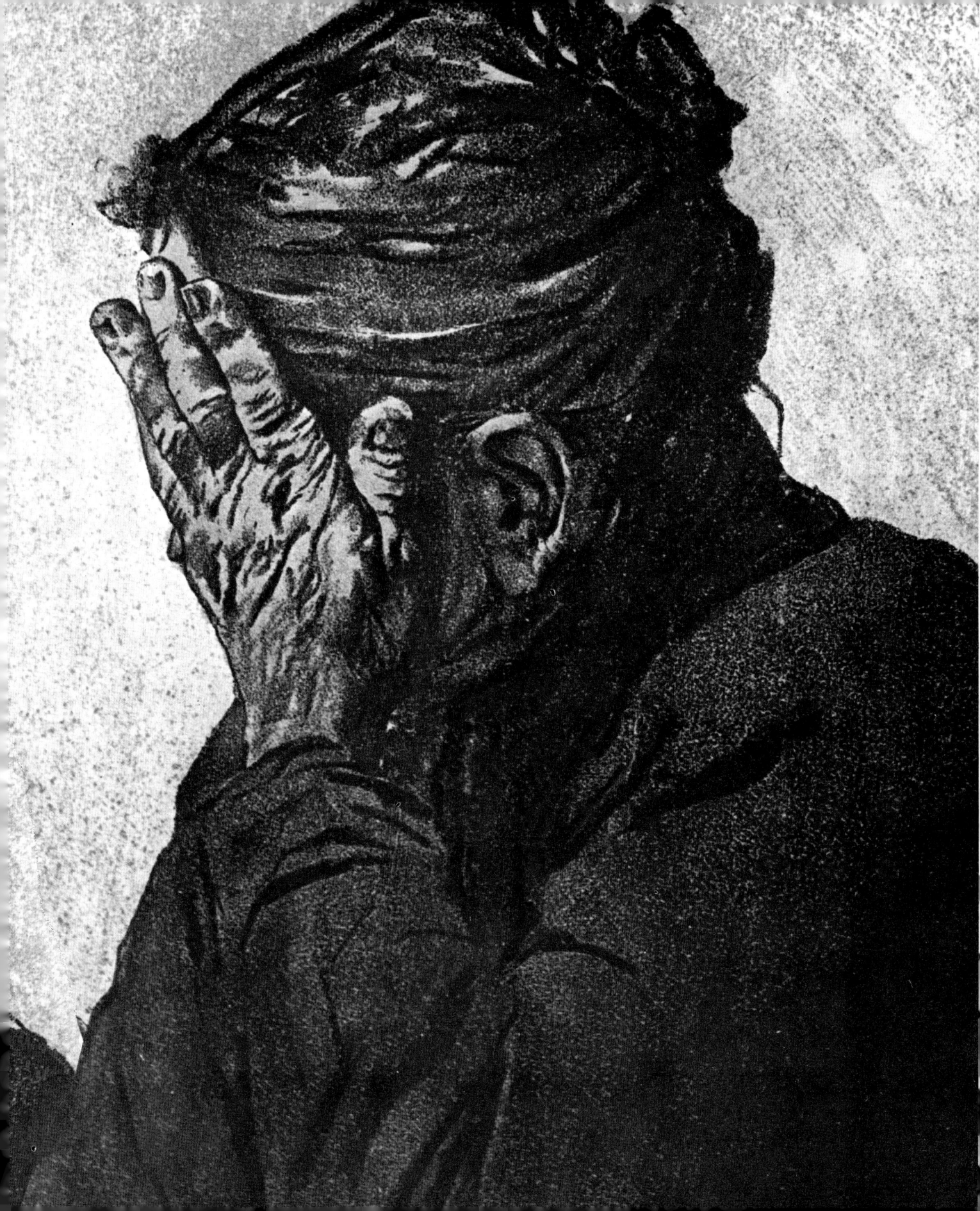

100 GERMANY

L. v Schaurath

Send gifts for our fighting troops

101 GERMANY

L. v Schaurath

Kaiser's and People's Fund for the Forces

102 RUSSIA

(.....?)

Everybody help our glorious soldiers! / Subscribe to 5½% War Loan

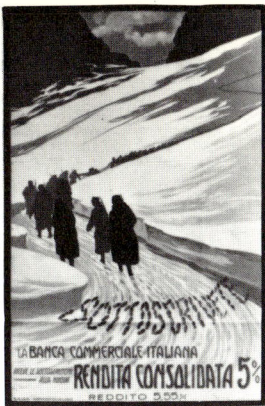

103 ITALY
Barchi
Subscribe;
5% Consolidated Stock

104 GERMANY

O. Weil
Mainz Gift Day /
Death and Danger in battle;
Wind and Weather for the lonely Watch;
God, be with you!
Your loved ones at home Hope and Pray.
We shall hold out!

DEBOUT DANS LA TRANCHÉE
QUE L'AURORE ÉCLAIRE, LE SOLDAT
RÊVE À LA VICTOIRE ET À SON FOYER.

POUR QU'IL PUISSE ASSURER L'UNE
ET RETROUVER L'AUTRE,

SOUSCRIVEZ
AU 3ᵉ EMPRUNT DE LA DÉFENSE NATIONALE

105 FRANCE
Lieut. Jean Droit
As dawn breaks over the trenches,
the soldier dreams of victory
— and of his hearth and home. /
So that he may achieve the one
and regain the other, subscribe to the
3rd National Defence Loan

106 FRANCE
Maurice Neumon
Soldier's Day, 1915

107 GREECE
Anonymous
Get back, Barbarian!

108 POLAND
Anonymous
*If you believe in God ... rally to
the colours of the Eagle of Pogoni!*

111 GERMANY
H.R. Erdt
The U-Boats are out!

ZA NAŠI SAMOSTATNOST!

HRR NA VRAHA!

ZA DEMOKRACII!

ČESKOSLOVENSKÁ ARMÁDA

109 *US* / (Czechoslovak Recruiting Office)

Vogtech Preissig
Down with the murderers!
Up with Democracy!

SEGÍTSETEK A DIADALMAS BÉKÉHEZ

**JEGYEZZÜNK
HADIKÖLCSÖNT**

110 HUNGARY
(.....?)
Help us to victorious peace / Buy war bonds
(The hand-axe was standard
army issue for use against barbed-wire)

112 BRITAIN
Frank Brangwyn

DO YOUR DUTY TO OUR BOYS AS
THEY ARE DOING THEIRS TO YOU
THE 1914 WAR SOCIETY WANTS TO GIVE EVERY DISABLED MAN A FAIR
CHANCE OF HONOURABLE INDEPENDENCE IN HEALTHY RURAL SURROUNDINGS

DONATIONS
LARGE or SMALL
BUT SEND NOW WHILE
YOU THINK OF IT
ADDRESS: 1914 WAR SOCIETY
28. DUKE ST, St JAMES'. W.

Opfertag

113 GERMANY
Richard Klein
Gift Day

FATEVI SOCI DELLA CROCE ROSSA

"LA PRESSE" MILANO

114 ITALY
M. Dudovich
Join the Red Cross

STAR & GARTER HOME
TOTALLY DISABLED SOLDIERS AND SAILORS

Haven

You can never repay these utterly broken men. But you can show your gratitude by helping to build this Home where they will be tenderly cared for during the rest of their lives. LET EVERY WOMAN SEND WHAT SHE CAN TODAY to the Lady Cowdray, Hon. Treasurer, The British Women's Hospital Fund, 21 Old Bond Street, W.

115 BRITAIN
Bernard Partridge

117 BRITAIN
G. Spencer Pryse

The NATION'S FUND FOR NURSES

A THANK-OFFERING

FROM THE BRITISH EMPIRE TO BRITISH NURSES

Contributions will be gratefully received by the Honorary Treasurer The Viscountess Cowdray at 16, Carlton House Ter., S.W.1. or 21, Old Bond Street, W.1.

Sammlung für ein Mutterhaus

Schwesternschaft „Haus Ostpreußen".

Geldspenden nehmen alle Banken an, sowie die Vaterl. Frauenvereine Ostpreußens.

116 GERMANY
Richard Pfeiffer
House of Mercy
Appeal

WANTED
25000 STUDENT NURSES

U.S. STUDENT NURSE RESERVE

ENROLL AT THE NEAREST RECRUITING STATION OF THE WOMAN'S COMMITTEE OF THE COUNCIL OF NATIONAL DEFENSE

118 USA
Milton Bancroft

IF I FAIL HE DIES

WORK for the RED CROSS

And attend the DULUTH AUTOMOBILE SHOW, Feb. 18 to 23, 1918.
ENTIRE PROCEEDS FOR THE RED CROSS.

119 USA
Rev. S. A. Kiek
and Arthur G. McCoy

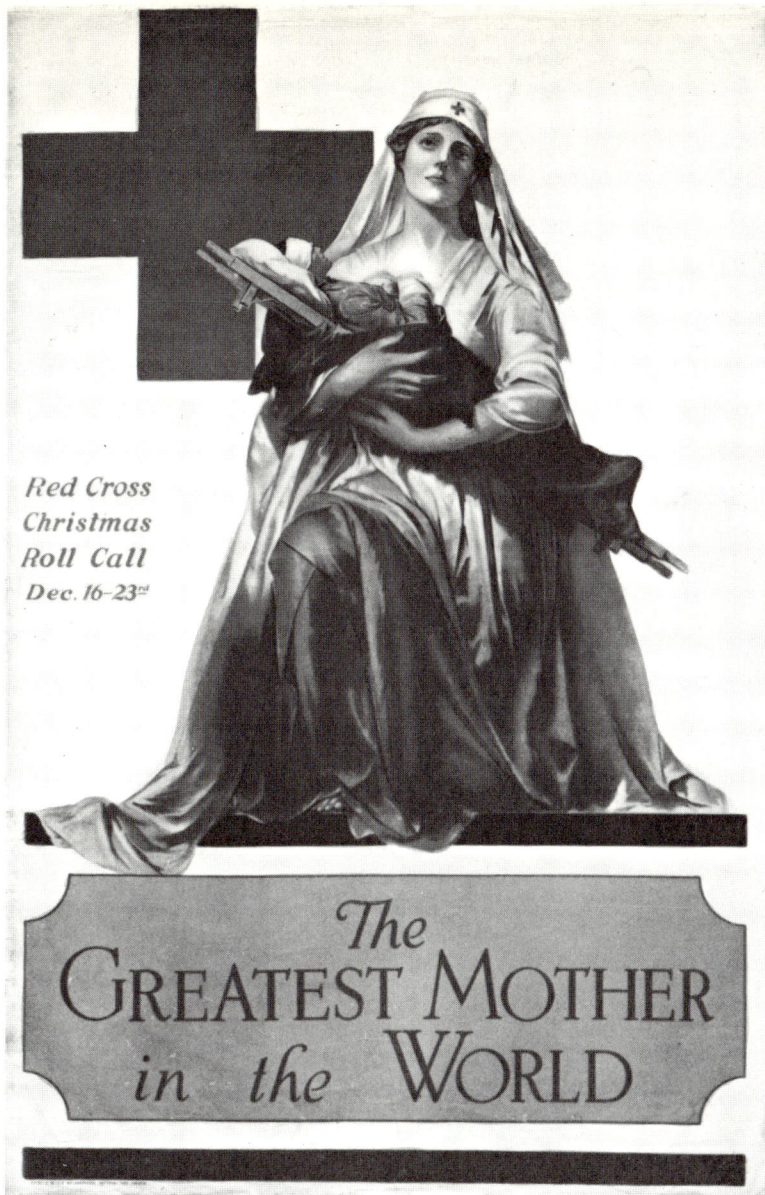

Red Cross
Christmas
Roll Call
Dec. 16–23rd

The
GREATEST MOTHER
in the WORLD

120 USA
A. E. Foringer

Schwesternspende
27. April 1918

Dankt
unsern Schwestern

123 GERMANY
R. Schuster Woldan
*Nurses' Flag Day /
Thank our nurses!*

FRANCE
ITALY
MALTA
GIBRALTAR
SALONICA

EGYPT
MESOPOTAMIA
HOLLAND
SWITZERLAND
RUSSIA

V.A.D.
NURSING MEMBERS, COOKS, KITCHEN·MAIDS,
CLERKS, HOUSE·MAIDS, WARD·MAIDS,
LAUNDRESSES, MOTOR·DRIVERS, ETC.
ARE URGENTLY NEEDED
APPLICATION TO BE MADE TO

122 BRITAIN
Joyce Dennys

We need you

121 USA
Albert Sterner

124 GERMANY
M. Werner
Help our war-blind

126 FRANCE
Adolphe Willette

128 FRANCE
Francisque Poulbot
*Vendée War-wounded
Welfare Day*

125 BRITAIN
Leon de Smet

127 GERMANY

Ludwig Hohlwein
Ludendorff Fund for War-Disabled

129 GERMANY

Anonymous
*War-wounded
Welfare Exhibition*

130 FRANCE

Georges Dorival
*The General Association
of War-wounded - for relief and
rehabilitation, placement, loans
and surgical care*

131 GREECE

Anonymous
The proud mother

..per la Patria i miei occhi! per la Pace il vostro denaro.

A. Ortelli

PRESTITO NAZIONALE
RENDITA CONSOLIDATA 5% NETTO
EMESSA a L. 86,50 per 100 NOMINALI
e REDDITO EFFETTIVO 5,78 per %

LE SOTTOSCRIZIONI SI RICEVONO!

PRESSO LE FILIALI DEGLI ISTITUTI DI EMISSIONE DI CREDITO ORDINA-
RIO-CASSE DI RISPARMIO-BANCHE POPOLARI E COOPERATIVE-DITTE
E SOCIETÀ BANCARIE-PARTECIPANTI AL CONSORZIO DEL PRESTITO

132 ITALY
A. Ortelli
For the Country
— my eyes;
for Peace
— your money

134 ITALY

A. Bonzagni
*Now it's your turn.
Subscribe!*

135 USA
Gordon Grant

136 GERMANY
Ferdy Horrmeyer
And YOUR duty?

133 GERMANY

W. Hammet
*I did this for you;
what are you doing
for me?*

137 USA
Anonymous

139 GERMANY
F. Stassen
Children in need /
German Children's Aid

140 FRANCE
Theophile Steinlen
The Devastated Aisne;
for the reconstruction of
destroyed homes

138 ITALY
M. Vinca
Our father has given
his life; will you
deny your money?

141 FRANCE
D. Charles Fouqueray
Friends of the
War Orphans

143 USA

Walter de Maris
*Have you room in your
heart for us?*

144 FRANCE

Jules Abel Faivre
*Charity Concert
announcement*

145 ITALY

Anonymous
*For a victorious return
subscribe to the Loan*

146 HUNGARY

Biró

Rebuild the villages of Saros
(Exhibition)

147 GERMANY

W. Krain

Give all — give plenty /
Help our border-refugees

148 GERMANY

M. Reifert
Alsace-Lorraine
Refugees Gift Day

149 FRANCE

Theophile Steinlen
Serbia Day

150 BRITAIN

John Hassall

151 FRANCE

G. Darcy
Help us!
(The return to Reims)

152 FRANCE

Theophile Steinlen
The Belgian are hungry
(Charity Lottery)

153 HUNGARY

Kádor
Please give us food! /
If we have no strength to work
we cannot give
you tools or clothing

154 BRITAIN

War Memorials
Exhibition

155 GERMANY

War Memorials
Exhibition

JOURNÉE DES RÉGIONS LIBÉRÉES

SONGEZ AUX FOYERS DÉT

ORPHELINAT
DESARMÉES

ASSURER AUX PETITS ORPHELINS::
LE FOYER ET LA TENDRESSE MATERNELLE
L'ÉDUCATION AU PAYS. UNE CARRIÈRE
APPROPRIÉE A CHAQUE ENFANT. LA
RELIGION DE LEURS PÈRES

FRANK BRANGWYN   W AVENUE PRESS LONDON. ENG.

157 FRANCE

Frank Brangwyn
*Army Orphanage /
To each child
motherly love, education,
an appropriate career
and the religion
of his parents ...*

Hönich
*Farmers, do your duty;
the towns are hungry!*

Bauern, tut euere Pflicht!
die Städte hungern

ENLIST

Fred Spear

159 USA
Fred Spear

160 USA
Howard Christy

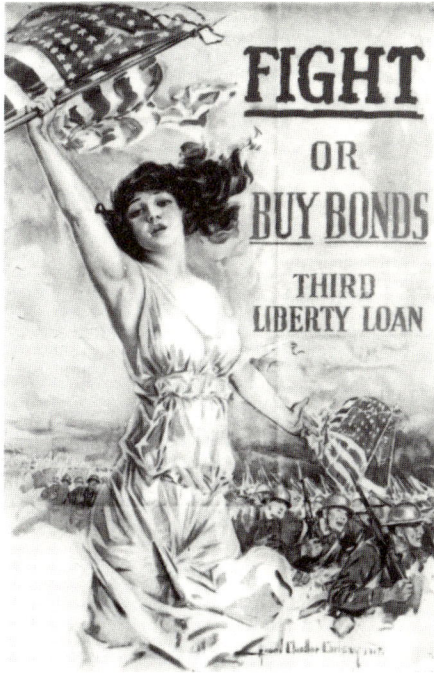

FIGHT OR BUY BONDS THIRD LIBERTY LOAN

161 USA
Babcock

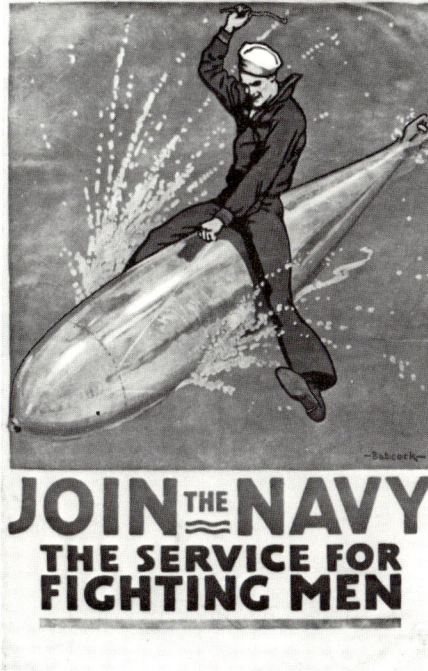

JOIN THE NAVY THE SERVICE FOR FIGHTING MEN

162 USA
Anonymous

ENLIST IN THE NAVY TO ARMS U.S. Navy Recruiting Station

163 FRANCE
" Sem "
*For the Freedom
of the World / Subscribe
to the National Loan*

POUR LA LIBERTÉ DU MONDE

BANQUE NATIONALE DE CRÉDIT

164 FRANCE
Anonymous
*America's answer
to the Huns*

LA RÉPONSE DE L'AMÉRIQUE AUX BOCHES

165 USA
John A. Coughlin

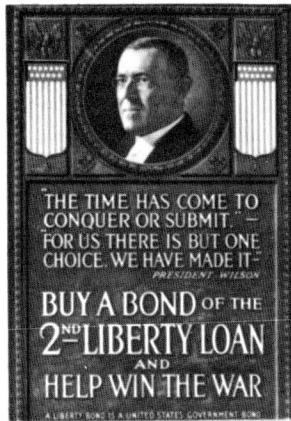

166 USA
Anonymous

167 USA
L. A. Shafer

168 USA
Walter Taylor

169 USA
Anonymous

171 USA
Anonymous

ND OFF DAY
W YORK NATIONAL GUARD

170 USA
Anonymous

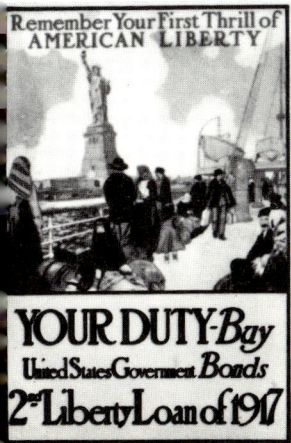

173 USA
L. N. Britton

Remember Your First Thrill of
AMERICAN LIBERTY

YOUR DUTY-Bay
United States Government Bonds
2ʳᵈ Liberty Loan of 1917

172 USA
Anonymous

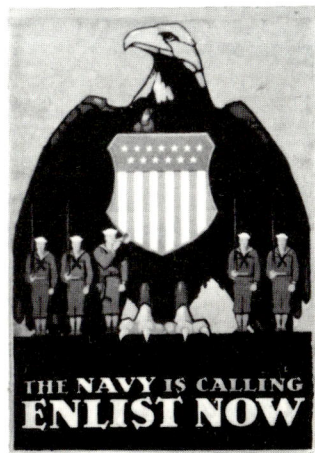

THE NAVY IS CALLING
ENLIST NOW

174 USA
John Norton

keep
these
off
the U.S.A
Buy more LIBERTY BONDS

MUST CHILDREN DIE AND MOTHERS PLEAD IN VAIN?

Buy More LIBERTY BONDS

175 USA
Raleigh

REMEMBER!
THE FLAG OF LIBERTY
SUPPORT IT!

BUY
U.S. Government Bonds
3rd. LIBERTY LOAN

177 ITALY

Varino
*Down with them,
soldier - people!*

giù forra
popolo-soldato!

Der ist Schuld,

Wenn Ihr noch kämpfen
und bluten müßt

Wenn Ihr noch entbehren
müßt

Wenn Ihr Kohle und Licht
sparen müßt

Wenn Ihr Lebensmittelkarten
und Bezugsscheine braucht

Wenn Ihr Eurer friedlichen
Arbeit noch nicht nachge-
hen könnt

Der Hauptfeind ist

England!

Darum
**Bleibt einig!
Bleibt stark!**
Damit verbürgt Ihr
**Deutschlands
Sieg!**

178 GERMANY

Otto Leonard

*His fault! / When, still compelled
to fight and bleed, /
when, suffering deprivation
everywhere, / you go without the coal
and warmth you need, /
with ration-cards and darkness for
your share, / with peace-time work no
longer to be done / someone guilty
there must be. /
England, the arch-enemy! /
Stand then, united, steadfastly! / For
Germany's sure cause will thus be won.*

"KNIGHTS OF THE AIR"

LOOK HINDENBURG! MY GERMAN HEROES!

179 BRITAIN

Howard Van Dusen

ONLY THE NAVY CAN STOP THIS

180 USA

W. A. Rogers

181 GERMANY

Paul Haase

If, with his army and
his hate, the enemy wins,
the workshops will
be empty. There will be
closed doors and
a tightening of belts.

183 GERMANY

Lucien Bernhard

Truth Abroad! /
We send out a
regular 10-language
news-sheet to the Press of the
neutral states.
Please help us by contributing
to friendly foreign relations!

182 USA

Ellsworth Young

184 USA

F. Strothmann

Unser Stolz

1914·15

Österreichische Motor-Batterie 30·5 cm Mörser.

ПОКУПАЙТЕ ВОЕННЫЙ 5½% ЗАЕМЪ ОБИЛІЕ СНАРЯДОВЪ-ЗАЛОГЪ ПОБѢДЫ.

185 AUSTRIA

H. Neumann
*Our Pride /
Austrian motorised 30.5 cm
Mortar Brigade*

186 RUSSIA

V. Varmanski
*Buy War Loan /
Ammunition means Victory!*

★ DAL PRESTITO LE ARMI E LA VITTORIA ★

BANCO DI ROMA
PRESTITO NAZIONALE
CONSOLIDATO 5%

S.A.I.G.-A.BARABINO·GENOVA

HELP
Deliver
the
Goods

DO IT NOW

187 ITALY

Caffonaro
Bank of Rome /
National Consolidated 5% Loan

188 USA

Paus

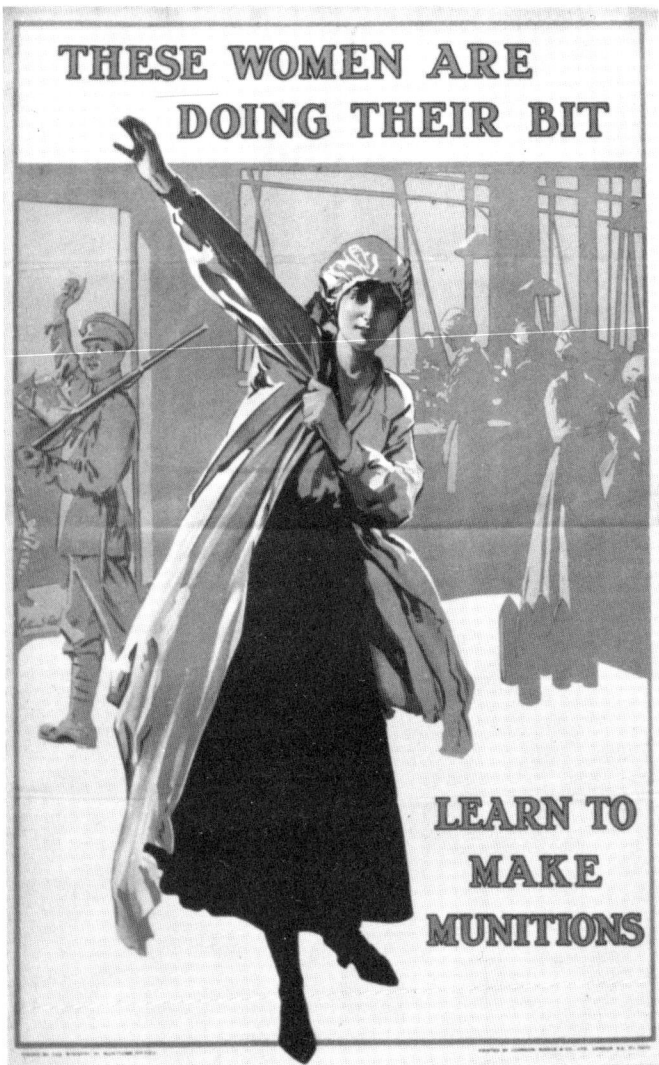

189 BRITAIN
Septimus E. Scott

190 GERMANY
Ferdy Horrmayer
*German women
- help us to victory!*

194 USA
Adolph Triedler

193 BRITAIN
Anonymous

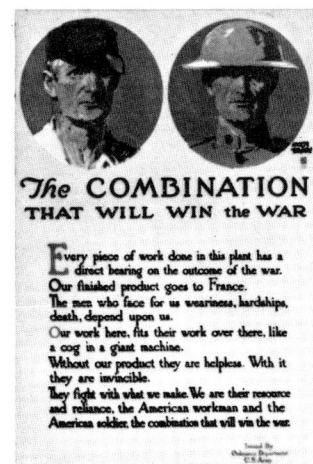

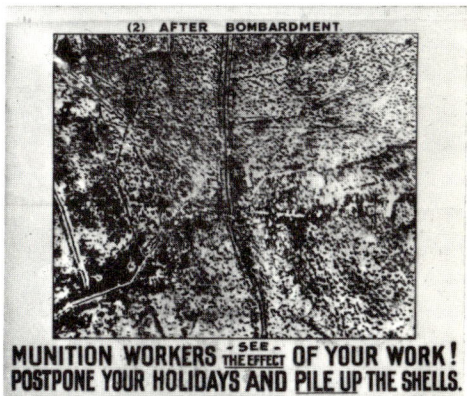

192 BRITAIN

191 RUSSIA

Anonymous
*Everything for the war! /
Subscribe to the 5½% War Loan*

195 GERMANY
Cay
*Through work to Victory
- through victory to Peace!*

196 BRITAIN
W. H. Scrivener

197 BRITAIN
Welsh

LES FOYERS DU SOLDAT

Y.M.C.A.

UNION FRANCO-AMERICAINE

VISA - 13684

ALBESSARD Édit - PARIS.

198 FRANCE
W. Philman Bunley
*Soldiers' Hostels
of the YMCA*

199 GERMANY
Max Antlers
*Kaiser's Birthday
Fund for German
Soldiers' Hostels
at the Front*

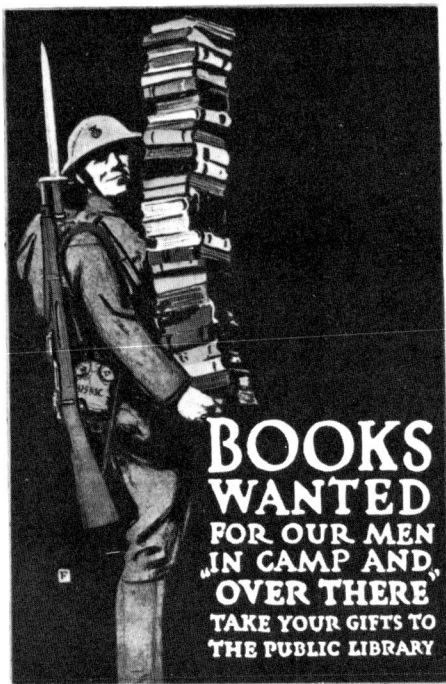

200 USA
C. B. Falls

201 GERMANY
Magda Koll
Gift Sunday

206 GERMANY
Weise
Good books make good men /
Whatever you give
— give books as well

207 GERMANY
A.K.
Send gifts for our boys from Baden below

208 BRITAIN
Frank Brangwyn

(Left)
203 GERMANY
Strover
Provide Soldiers' Hostels at the Front!

(Right)
204 GERMANY
Magda Koll
Help Bremen build 4 Soldiers' hostels

205 FRANCE
Georges Dorival
Soldiers' Hostels of the YMCA

BRITAIN
ank Brangwyn

209 FRANCE
P. Renouard
*Invalided Soldiers' Aid /
A call to every heart*

210 GERMANY
Max Antlers
*German Forces Book Fund /
We need books, please give money*

Volksspende
für die deutschen
Kriegs- und Zivil-
Gefangenen

211 GERMANY
Ludwig Hohlwein
German Prisoners' Fun

"MACHINE GUN CORPS, PRISONERS OF WAR FUND"

ΒΟΥΛΓΑΡΟΙ ΑΙΧΜΑΛΩΤΟΙ

LE VÊTEMENT DU PRISONNIER DE GUERRE

RATTACHÉ A LA ✚ FRANÇAISE

63, Avenue des Champs-Elysées, PARIS

Cette Œuvre a pour but de vêtir les prisonniers français et belges, militaires ou civils, internés en Allemagne.

Il faut aux prisonniers militaires des vêtements chauds; un grand nombre d'entre eux, captifs depuis l'été, en sont complètement dépourvus.

D'autre part, les prisonniers civils, pris « tels qu'ils se trouvaient » dans les régions envahies françaises et belges, souffrent particulièrement du manque de vêtements. Il y a parmi eux des femmes, des enfants, des vieillards!

Tous, militaires ou civils, sont insuffisamment nourris et reçoivent avec joie des envois d'alimentation.

Aussi adressons-nous un pressant appel à toutes les bonnes volontés, à tous les cœurs charitables. Les envois de l'Œuvre parviennent régulièrement à nos prisonniers, qu'il s'agisse de vêtements ou de nourriture.

Nous espérons que chacun voudra bien nous aider dans cette œuvre de pitié, soit par des **Souscriptions**, si minimes soient-elles, soit par des **Dons en nature** — Chandails, Tricots, Chemises, Caleçons, Chaussettes, Mouchoirs, Tabac, Chocolat, Sucre, Conserves; — tout sera accepté avec la plus grande reconnaissance.

LES DONS, soit en espèces, soit en nature, sont reçus
AU SIÈGE DE L'ŒUVRE, 63, Avenue des Champs-Elysées.

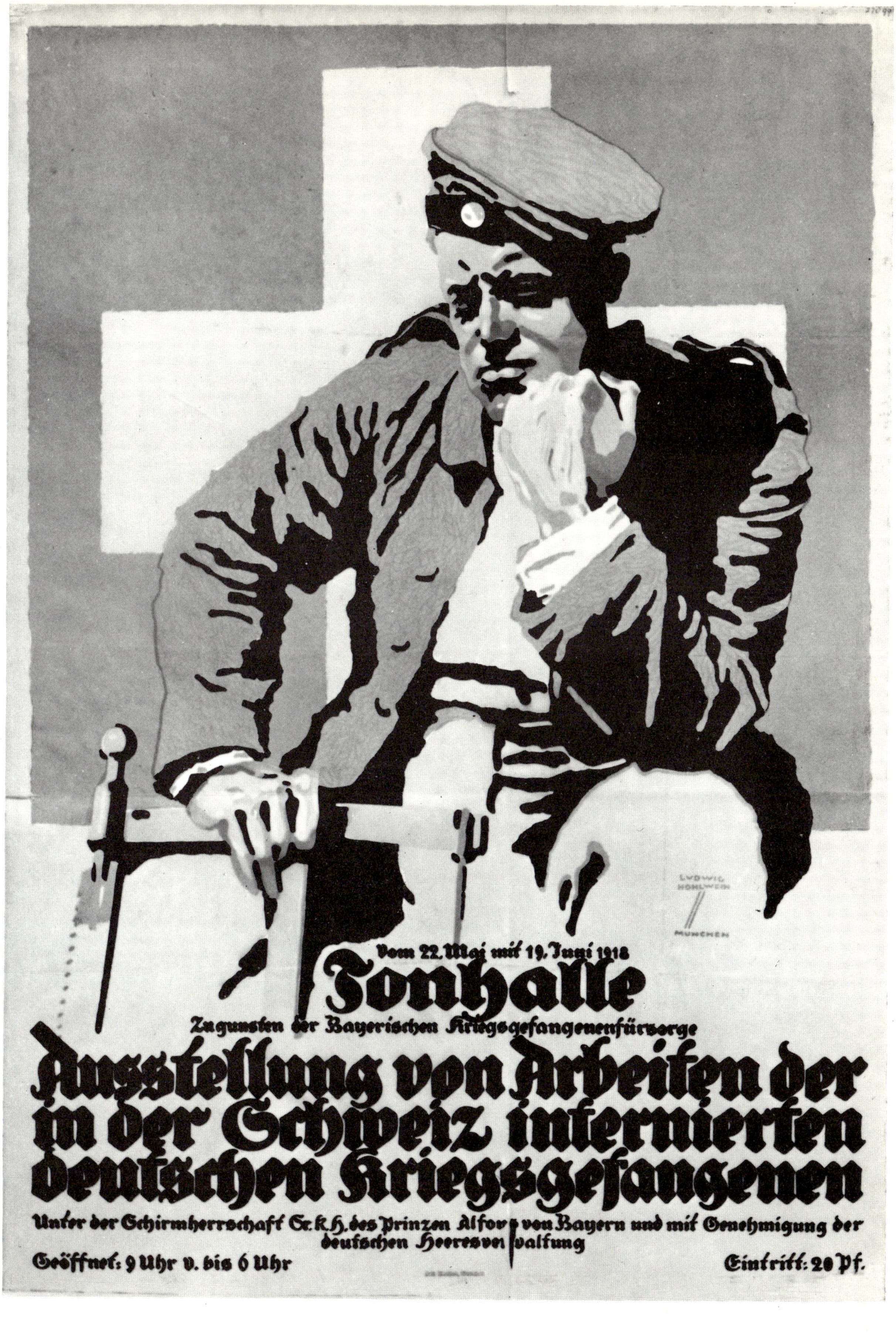

216 GERMANY
Ludwig Hohlwein
Exhibition of work by German internees in Switzerland

217 GERMANY
Oswald Polte
Gold and Jewellery Week
(State purchasing campaign)

218 GERMANY
Jupp Wiertz
Women — give your hair!

221 GERMANY
C. Strohmeyer
Paper! Bring it to the
collection centre

219 GERMANY
C. Strohmeyer
Collect bottles!

220 GERMANY
Winckel
Bring your money /
Hasten peace /
Bring back happiness

222 GERMANY
Louis Oppenheim
Aluminium, copper,
brass, nickel, tin / Bring it,
the army needs it

Zeichnet Kriegsanleihe

Die Zeit ist hart, aber der Sieg ist sicher

223 GERMANY
R.B.
*Times are hard,
but victory
is certain*

U.S. FOOD
ADMINISTRATION

EAT MORE
CORN, OATS AND RYE
PRODUCTS — FISH
AND POULTRY — FRUITS,
VEGETABLES AND POTATOES
BAKED, BOILED AND
BROILED FOODS

EAT LESS
WHEAT, MEAT, SUGAR AND FATS

TO SAVE FOR THE ARMY
AND OUR ASSOCIATES

226 GERMANY
Julius Gipkens
*Collect fruit stones /
Let your children
take them to school,
or send them
to the nearest
Collection Centre*

228 USA
Crawford Young

225 BRITAIN
U.J.B.

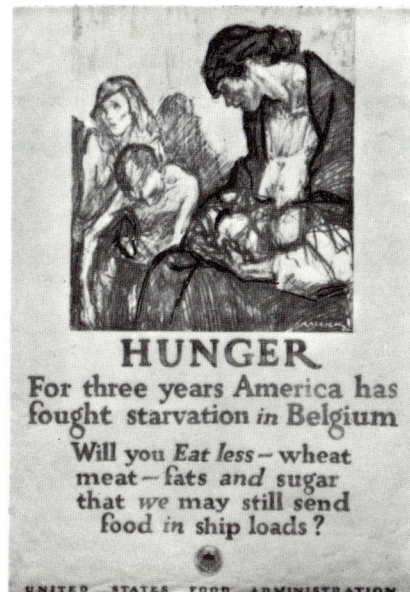

227 USA
Raleigh

Altonaer Kriegshilfetag

29. Sept. 1917

Ausstellung v. Gemüse u. Obst aus Kleingärten vom 28. Sept. bis 1. Oktober im Kaiserhof. Veranstalter: Kleingarten-Kommission d. Stadt Altona und Altonaer Kriegshilfe.

229 GERMANY
W. Battermann
Altona War Aid Day

We risk our lives to bring you food. It's up to you not to waste it.

"A Message from our Seamen"

231 BRITAIN
Harvey Dunne

232 GERMANY
Julius Gipkens
*Collect fruit-stones
for oil production*

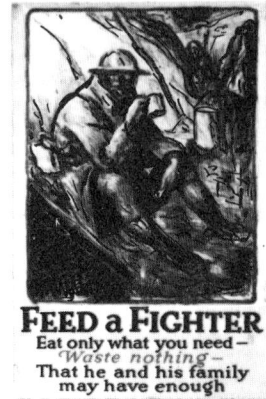

233 USA
Wallace Morgan

238 FRANCE
Marthe Picard (16 yrs)
Eat less meat. Conserve our livestock

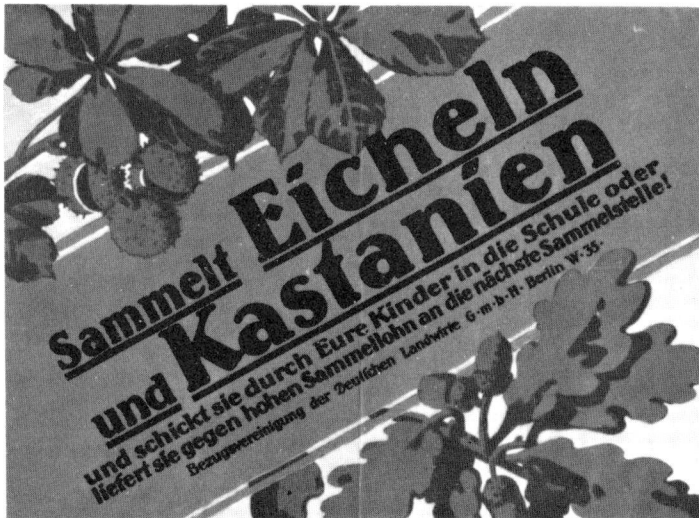

236 GERMANY
Julius Gipkens
Collect acorns and chestnuts

237 USA
H.G. Gawthorn

234 GERMANY
Anonymous
Collect apple and pear-peelings

235 USA
Edward Penfield

239 GERMANY
Lucien Bernhard
*The potato has saved Germany; it will go on doing so /
Plant more potatoes; plant them better*

240 USA
(.....?)

241 GERMANY

Walter Ditz

*Shine out, holy flame,
shine out /
shine through the darkn.
for the Fatherland*

Frank Brangwyn
*Army Orphanage /
To each child
motherly love, education,
an appropriate career,
and the religion
of his parents ...*

ORPHELINAT DES ARMÉES

ASSURER AUX PETITS ORPHELINS::
LE FOYER ET LA TENDRESSE MATERNELLE
L'ÉDUCATION AU PAYS. UNE CARRIÈRE
APPROPRIÉE A CHAQUE ENFANT. LA
RELIGION DE LEURS PÈRES